RESTLESS

The Memoirs of Labor and Consumer Activist Esther Peterson

The Memoirs of Labor and Consumer Activist Esther Peterson

ESTHER PETERSON
with WINIFRED CONKLING

CARING
PUBLISHING

519 C STREET, NE • WASHINGTON, DC

© 1995 by Esther Peterson

All rights reserved. No part of this book may be reproduced in any form or by any electronic or mechanical means, including information storage and retrieval systems, without written permission from the publisher, except in the case of brief quotations embodied in articles or reviews. For information, contact Caring Publishing, 519 C Street, NE, Washington, DC 20002-5809.

Printed in the United States of America.

Library of Congress Catalog Number 95-067570
ISBN 1-886450-02-1   *casebound*
ISBN 1-886450-03-X   *perfect bound*

All photos, unless otherwise credited, are courtesy of Esther Peterson.

Dedication

No one can do what I have done without a lot of help.
I dedicate this book to those who are often forgotten, but who
have allowed me to enjoy my life as well as my work—
my housekeepers, my babysitters, and of course, my family.

A Tribute to Esther Peterson
by Jimmy Carter . . . . *i*

Introduction . . . . *iii*

1. The Cowslips Are in Bloom 1
2. Life Beyond the Valley 17
3. Bread and Roses 33
4. Disturbing the Peace 51
5. Uprooted 69
6. "Esther, Where Have You Been?" 93
7. "The Most Dangerous Thing Since Genghis Khan" 119
8. Put Up or Shut Up 137
9. Back to the White House 159
10. Will "Made in America" Become A Warning Label? 171
11. Looking Back 183

A Tribute to Esther Peterson

*On the Occasion of Her Receiving the
Presidential Medal of Freedom*

> THE PRESIDENT OF THE UNITED STATES OF AMERICA
> AWARDS THIS PRESIDENTIAL MEDAL OF FREEDOM
> TO ESTHER PETERSON
>
>
>
> ONCE GOVERNMENT'S HIGHEST RANKING WOMAN,
> ESTHER PETERSON STILL RANKS HIGHEST AMONG CONSUMER
> ADVOCATES. SHE HAS ADVISED PRESIDENTS AND THE PUBLIC, AND
> HAS WORKED FOR LABOR AND BUSINESS ALIKE, ALWAYS KEEPING THE
> RIGHTS OF ALL AMERICANS TO KNOW AND TO BE TREATED FAIRLY AS
> HER HIGHEST PRIORITY. EVEN HER STAUNCHEST FOES RESPECT
> HER INTEGRITY AND ARE WARMED BY HER GRACE
> AND SINCERE CONCERN.

You may be surprised that in the citation the word "foes" is mentioned in relation to this lovely American, but she has made some foes. And I would guess, knowing her, that she's prouder of the foes she has made…than even some of the friends she has. She has never been afraid to address difficult issues even at the expense on occasion of personal harmony with those about whom she cares. She serves others with her entire dedicated life.

She's come to the inner circles of the White House in a major position during these last few years to work with me to make sure that the average American is not cheated, that they are told the truth, that they are treated fairly, and that when they go into the marketplace they can have some inner sense of trust in the free enterprise system which she has served so well. She's a delightful person, a person with charm, a person who makes deep friendships and deep commitments. And her deepest commitment has been to those who don't know her and who will probably never see her or maybe not even hear her voice. She serves those who are most deprived and has done that with her whole life.

I love her personally, and I congratulate her on receiving this award, the Medal of Freedom of our country.

—President Jimmy Carter
January 16, 1981

Introduction

"Do what is right, let the consequences follow." This is the theme of one of the hymns I sang in the Mormon church as a child, but to me it means much more than that. If I were to select a single phrase that I consider key to leading a meaningful life, that might well be it.

To do right and to accept the consequences of your actions requires that you make a choice about how you will lead your life rather than simply accepting what comes your way. I admire people who refuse to settle for things the way they are and struggle to make them a bit better. Perhaps that is because I come from a long line of malcontents. My great grandparents weren't satisfied with their lot in Denmark, so they came to America to build a better life. They made one, settling in Utah along with other penniless pioneers of the Mormon Church. I seem to have inherited from them a restlessness and a willingness to rock the boat a bit when the need arises.

Over the years, I've learned that it's not always easy to do what is right. In my experience, honesty has helped guide me, along with a lot of support from my husband, Oliver. For a time, it wasn't even clear to me that Oliver was Mr. Right. Oh, I knew I loved him, but he was a socialist who drank coffee and smoked a pipe, and I was a conservative Mormon Republican from Utah. In the end, I trusted my heart and rejected the rules about what I was supposed to do. I can't imagine how my life would have turned out if I hadn't had the courage to accept that I had fallen in love.

My Oliver gave me the strength to work for change and to disturb the peace at times. As a young woman, I helped to organize the workers, usually women, in the sweatshops in New England in the 1930s and in Utah and the South in the 1940s. Later I challenged the status quo by getting President Kennedy to look into the traditional and legally circumscribed status of American women and by working as the nation's first appointed consumer advocate. I take a lot of pride in the work I did to get equal pay for equal work, to increase the minimum wage and to expand its coverage to the left-out women, and to help secure passage of important consumer legislation. I know that a lot of people do not recognize my name, and they don't know the names of the courageous members of Congress who battled to get needed legislation passed into law, but I must say, I believe our efforts have made the nation a bit more fair and honest.

I hesitate to take even partial credit for so many of the projects I've worked on because I've had so much help from others. In every struggle, whether trying to organize a union or trying to get appropriate labeling on foods in the grocery store, we always tried to compromise and to draw the circle wider to bring more people in. I learned that from Eleanor Roosevelt. When we were working on President Kennedy's Commission on the Status of Women, she would say, "Mrs. Peterson, you must always compromise, but compromise upward."

A willingness to push for change and a willingness to compromise: these things I hope I leave as a legacy to my grandchildren. But I must remind them of a lesson taught to me by a geology professor at Brigham Young University, who took his class into Provo Canyon to show us the faults that had built the Wasatch Range. "Those layers upon layers of stone took millions of years to build up," he said, "so be patient about making change. But please, students," he went on, "don't be too patient." I echo his words to the next generation: When it comes to making the world a little bit better, don't be too patient.

Chapter 1

The Cowslips Are in Bloom

I was 12 years old when I witnessed my first strike. The year was 1918 and the railway workers in Provo, Utah, went out on strike for an eight-hour workday on the Union Pacific line. As a child I didn't know much about this particular strike, but I knew about the evils of unions. I had been told that all labor leaders were dangerous people, real troublemakers, filled with socialist ideas about unions achieving a workers' rebellion. I had learned that the letters IWW stood for "I Won't Work," rather than the International Workers of the World, a leftist union. The entire community had been taught the same lessons: work was an almost sacred duty and obedience to a higher authority—whether the foreman or God Himself—was the bedrock of an ordered society. I had heard family members talk about the newly triumphant Bolsheviks in Russia and the "Red Menace" inherent in American unionism; I knew these outsiders had no place in our quiet town.

When I was a child, my family took in Brigham Young University (BYU) students as boarders to help make ends meet. Railroad officials came to the university to recruit strikebreakers, tempting them with a salary of $10 a day, magnificent pay in those days. The students always needed money to pay for their education, and $10 could cover the cost of room and board for more than two weeks at that time. If the strikers didn't want to work, why shouldn't these men take their jobs?

On the first day that the students went to work as strikebreakers, my sister Algie offered to drive them to the roundhouse in Salt

Lake. We had a new Dodge, an open touring car, and we used any excuse possible to justify a ride. I begged Algie to let me come along, and she eventually agreed.

When we first left town I felt proud to be driving in a flashy new car, loaded with men who would help to put the strikers in their place. But those feelings disappeared when we approached the crowd at the roundhouse. We had to drive the car through a thick crowd; there was a chaotic mix of picketers and police at the gate. Policemen on horses held back the strikers to clear a path for our car to get through.

At one point the car stopped and a woman, one of the strikers' wives, stared at me. She had two little children by her side, clinging to her. Her gaze penetrated me as she said, "Why are you doing this to us?"

I knew something was wrong, but I didn't understand her despair. I didn't appreciate how she must have felt as she watched carloads of hearty young men move in to take her husband's work. My sister continued to drive the workers to the roundhouse each day, but I never again went along.

I couldn't stop thinking about that woman's face. I thought about her a lot when my mind would wander at church. I was part of a good Mormon family; we regularly attended the Provo Fourth Ward of the Latter Day Saints (Mormons). I used to love singing, but I paid little attention to the words. I don't know exactly why, but the Sunday after the strike, the meaning of the words jumped up at me as I was singing at Sunday school. I felt uneasy as I sang the words of an old Mormon hymn:

> Have I done any good in the world today?
> Have I helped anyone in need?
> Have I cheered up the sad, and made someone feel glad?
> If not, I have failed indeed.

I just kept thinking about that woman's face. Had I failed her? I wondered if we had done something wrong when we pushed our way through those strikers. I wasn't sure. That was more than 75 years ago, but it seems like yesterday. Over the years I have served as a labor organizer, a federal bureaucrat, and an aide for three US presidents, and I have often thought of that striker's wife standing in a crowd asking, "Why?"

That strike was my first exposure to workers' poverty. Throughout my childhood, I had been taught that the rich were rewarded by God—"He prospers who deserves to prosper,"—and that the Mormon Church takes care of its poor. God blesses the millionaires, but He doesn't require that they pay their workers a living wage. Who was I to question the natural order?

I was the fifth of Lars and Annie Eggertsen's six children. We all grew up in a big brick house on North University Avenue in Provo, Utah. In our Mormon community, living clean was the code: Dutiful Mormons strictly adhered to the Word of Wisdom, a revelation set forth in 1834 by prophet Joseph Smith that prohibited the Saints from partaking of tobacco, alcohol, or "hot drinks," particularly tea and coffee. Mormons were not only expected to follow the four "don'ts," we were to sing about them: "Tea and coffee and tobacco we despise...we are seeking to be great and good and wise." I never questioned the reason for these prohibitions, and it wasn't until years later that I learned from a professor at Brigham Young University that the Mormon leader, Brigham Young, prohibited these luxuries because he didn't want the Saints to use their cash to buy them; the early settlers needed all the money they had to buy seeds.

Growing up, our weeks were filled with church on Sunday and meetings nearly every day of the week, including Relief Society meetings for the women, Priesthood meetings for the men, Mutual Improvement Society meetings for young men and women, and Primary for the young kids after school. Church activities filled our days, and we believed all we were taught. I worked hard at being "good." As a child, when I would nibble from my plate before my father said grace, I would keep my mouth open during the blessing, hoping that some of the prayer might reach the food in my tummy and keep it from choking me.

Despite the time spent on religious activity, my family wasn't iron-clad in its enforcement of the religious rules. My parents were both great coffee drinkers. Quite simply, my parents never accepted that a hard-working, self-respecting Dane could go through life without a good, strong cup of coffee to start the morning. My parents also indulged in a second cup in the middle of the afternoon, and I assume the same principle applied. My mother used to say, "I cannot believe in a God that would not let me drink my coffee." My parents broke the rules, but the children weren't allowed to have any coffee, of course. I didn't taste coffee until I was 23 years old.

The Relief Society rotated the location of its meetings from house to house. My mother's meeting was always the most successful, and the ward bishop always came. Mormons drink postum, a drink made from cracked wheat and served like coffee. "Sister Eggertsen," the bishop would say, "you make the best postum in the entire ward." My mother would murmur something about putting eggshells in the grounds, but she didn't mention the spoonful of real coffee she added to the brew.

Another religious indiscretion involved playing games with the full, 52-card deck of playing cards, which were forbidden by the church as too indolent, not to mention their use in sinful games of chance. We used real playing cards to play *sevincel*, a Danish form of bridge that, if played correctly, involves a lot of banging on the table and loud laughter. During these games we kept an innocent deck of rook cards nearby, just in case a ward teacher or neighbor stopped by, perhaps to check on the noisy laughter. The forbidden deck could easily be swept under the tablecloth until the danger of discovery had passed. We never really considered these minor violations of church rules as wrong. My father, the pillar of rectitude in the issues that really counted, would dismiss the doubts: "This is a family matter," he would say.

One of the beliefs of the Mormon religion is that women who are unmarried will never reach the highest order in Heaven unless they go through a ceremony to be either "sealed" or married to a man. Because my father was superintendent of schools in Provo, many spinster teachers would ask to be sealed to him. He could have as many women sealed to him as he wanted; it was a no-obligation ritual, though in my mind this has always seemed like celestial polygamy.

My father would come home on the days he had been sealed and say to my mother, "Annie, I have another helper for you."

"Why can't you get me help here on Earth? I won't need any more help in Heaven," came her reply. I don't really know if my parents believed in the sealing ritual or not, but I know my father went through with it, and he made a lot of women happy because of it.

Although many people associate Mormonism with polygamy or plural marriage, our family had only one polygamist, my Aunt Sarah. Some people joke about the days of polygamy—"polygamy is better than monotony"—but I will never forget hearing stories of the pain and dread that polygamy brought to the lives of many young Mormon girls.

My father's sister Sarah married into polygamy with one of the important church officials, Benjamin Cluff. She told me tales of her wedding night: Her husband had sex with her, then he left and went down the hall, and she heard him having sex twice more with two other wives. Before leaving he told her, "It is my duty." She had no choice but to accept it. She later told me that it was all part of "the sex burden that women have to tolerate." The church did not end officially sanctioned plural marriages until 1890. In the early days the church leaders used the excuse that there were more women than men, but I believe polygamy was little more than a way of giving official sanction to infidelity.

I poke fun at some of the traditions of my community, but Provo was a fine place to grow up. One of my fondest memories is of the July 24 celebration of Pioneer Day, recognizing the founding of the state of Utah. We had a big parade that included people pulling handcarts, representing the original settlers. My grandparents on my father's side were among those first settlers in Utah in the late 1840s; they had walked across the plains to the Promised Land, a claim that carries the same weight as having a family that arrived on the Mayflower.

In the parade, the pretty girls from each ward were chosen to ride on the fancy floats, wearing beautiful clothes and waving to the crowd. I always rode on the haywagon that followed behind, filled with lots of kids and a sign saying, "Utah's Best Crop." Not being chosen one of the pretty ones never really bothered me; I never considered myself attractive enough to qualify for a space on the fancy float. I loved Pioneer Day because I was always given a shiny nickel to spend however I wanted. As I recall, I always indulged in a double-scoop vanilla ice cream cone.

In Provo most men farmed alfalfa or tended fruit orchards; the women raised big broods of children and put up food for the winter. Life seemed so simple and safe. Some of my warmest childhood memories involve peeling peaches with my brothers and sisters as my father read poetry and short stories to us.

My father was a calm, quiet, loving man with an easy manner. He always did what was needed, almost without thinking. He and I once went to Springville for the Memorial Day celebration. The appointed speaker didn't show up, so the host asked my father to substitute. Without any preparation, he climbed the platform and made a stirring speech. When we got home and he told Mother, she was furious; he had been wearing a pair of pants with a very visible patch on the seat.

I was always very proud of my father. I didn't really understand what it meant to be superintendent of schools; I assumed it meant that he owned the schools. When I would get in trouble with other kids at school, I would sometimes threaten that they better be careful because my father owned the school.

My father always noticed the little things. When we were doing chores, he would pause, look toward the pasture, and say, "Look, Esther, the cowslips are in bloom." He didn't allow the small things to go unnoticed.

He respected nature and was comfortable with it. When it came to teaching us about sex, he was never afraid to explain the natural order of the barnyard. He would ask me, "Esther, do you want to come with me when I take the cow to the bull?"

"What for?"

"So he can put his seeds in her to make a calf." Sex wasn't something we had to be taught formally; it was simply a part of life.

In the same way, learning about menstruation wasn't a traumatic event for me or my sisters. One day when the family was down at the lake, I saw blood running down my sister's leg and asked what had happened. Without nervousness or apology my parents explained that it was nothing to worry about; my sister was just having her "monthly" and that one day I would, too.

Attitudes about sex and farming and the value of work we almost picked up by accident just by being around my father. But certain lessons we were taught explicitly and directly. For example, in the dry mountain air we had to water all our plants. Neighboring families shared a single irrigation ditch, and one of my jobs was to get up at 4:00AM on days it was our family's turn to fix the dam so the water would flow down to our corn and potatoes and carrots. After I switched the dam, I had to go down to the end of every row to make sure the water reached the end. I would then dam off the water so that it would flow down the next ditch or row. If I wasn't paying attention, the area would flood and my father would be furious that we were wasting water. "You're watering weeds, not vegetables," he would say.

During these lectures my father would remind me, "Esther, always get the water running where *you* want it to go." Keep the water moving; whenever you see it going where it shouldn't go, get in there and change it. That's an important lesson that I've thought of a number of times in my life. You have some control over how things happen in your life, but only if you keep the water moving where you want it to go.

My mother, Annie, was always very busy, cooking and cleaning and sewing and supervising six children, as well as up to 12 additional boarders. I must say she taught me to appreciate the economic value of women's work. We had a big house, but not a lot of money. My family wouldn't have been able to afford to put the kids through college and maintain our standard of living without my mother's constant contributions.

My mother also gave me my first consumer education while shopping at Garrett's Grocery Store on University Avenue. I learned about textiles from our visits to the Utah Woolen Mills. I learned about food production from living on a farm. The family's chickens produced our eggs; our cows provided the milk and butter; we even went to the flour mill to see the wheat we had grown ground into flour.

Although they were both very busy, my parents always took time to be alone together in the morning. The rule was that my brothers and sisters and I couldn't come into the kitchen as long as the door was closed. After my parents had time to enjoy a quiet cup of coffee together, they opened the door and we all came in and ate breakfast.

I enjoyed special times with my mother in the kitchen in the mornings. There was a space between the big coal stove and the wall; I stood in the nook, where it was warm and I could be near her as she cooked oatmeal and eggs for breakfast. I was out of the way, but still close. I learned a lot about cooking by standing there and watching her.

My mother was a very handsome woman with beautiful hair that she wore in a big bun on the top of her head. She was strong; she had no trouble carrying a big basket of wet clothes to the clothesline. My mother also had the emotional strength to do whatever was needed to help her family.

When my father became ill when I was a child, my mother took a job as matron of the Poor Folks Farm. In those days, all the old people who had no one to take care of them went to the home. It didn't have a good reputation for cleanliness or care, but my mother changed that. She spent most of her days there, and we spent a great number of afternoons there helping out. I will never forget the stench of the mattresses soaked in urine and infested with bedbugs. We had to drag the mattresses outside and throw them against the side of the hill in the sun. Then my brother and I had to put the legs of the beds in pails filled with kerosene to keep the bed bugs from climbing back into the beds. The tasks were often unpleasant, and my mother wasn't paid much, but I was always very proud of how she turned the place around.

My grandparents didn't live far from Provo. My mother's mother, Grandma Mette Marie Nielsen, lived in Pleasant Grove, a little farming town north of Provo. She raised my mother to be proud of her Danish heritage; she warned us not to "let our Danish side down." Grandma Nielsen extended her Danish pride to the neighborhood children as well: She would stand outside her house when they walked to school, pulling aside and inspecting the children of Danish immigrants, washing faces and combing hair as necessary. "I don't want anybody calling us 'dumb, dirty Danes,'" she would say. At that time, Pleasant Grove was called "Little Denmark" because there were so many immigrants. For the longest time, when I heard grown-ups talking about the Old Country, I thought they were talking about Pleasant Grove.

My grandparents on both sides of the family were Danes who joined the Mormon Church in Denmark. They found the magical, New World gospel of the young Mormon missionaries a refreshing new vision of how to change their lives.

In Denmark my grandmother Mette Marie lived with her widowed father on a *gärd*, a huge family farm. My grandmother expected to become matriarch of the farm, but her father remarried and she lost her status as mistress of the *gärd*. The house keys she had worn on her apron were literally passed to her new—and most unwelcome—stepmother. The promise of a new life in America sounded more appealing than life at home without an estate to manage, so she and her husband and their five children crossed the Atlantic in search of a better life. My mother, Annie, was seven years old.

According to family lore, they crossed the Atlantic Ocean in steerage, surviving on the hard breads, cheese, and cured meats they brought along. My grandmother told me how hard it was to feed her own children from the big hampers of food when there were other children of parents with less foresight begging her for food. She shared what she could, but she had to take care of her family first.

My father's parents came to the United States from Denmark separately, each looking for a future. They joined the great Mormon handcart companies, the nearly penniless Saints who walked across the plains and the Rockies to Zion, working like human oxen to pull the handcarts that carried all their possessions. On their trek, the pioneers sang the anthem of their new faith:

> Come, come ye Saints, no toil nor labor fear,
> But with joy wend your way.
> Though hard to you this journey may appear,
> Grace shall be as your day.
> 'Tis better far for us to strive,
> Our useless cares from us to drive;
> Do this, and joy your hearts will swell—
> All is well! All is well!

Grandma and Grandpa Eggertsen met on the trail and fell in love. When they reached Salt Lake City, I am told, they were married by Brigham Young, the great prophet himself.

These two families united when my parents met as students at Brigham Young Academy, which later became the university. Mother was one of the first women to attend the academy; she studied to be a teacher, and Dad studied accounting. After graduation, my father went to Denmark on his religious mission, where he literally dreamed about marrying Annie. When he returned he courted her, and they married. I don't really know much about their relationship or early marriage; they were both very private people who kept such stories to themselves.

At the time I was growing up, the world seemed so fixed and secure. But now, as I look back, I realize that those times too were filled with doubt. In particular I remember the confusion stirred up by my brother, Luther, the rogue and rebel, who always interjected his opinions into the conversation across the big dining room table. Luther used to discuss Darwin and his theories of evolution over Sunday dinner. At the time, evolution provoked quite a bit of debate. The church—and my parents—did not accept the theory of evolution; they would not accept that God allowed us to come from monkeys. Still, my parents always tolerated different opinions.

During one such conversation, the discussion focused on the controversial 1897 book, *Theology of an Evolutionist*, by Lyman

Abbott. Luther had been reading it aloud to me; I was about 13 years old, and I looked up to my wise older brother. In the heat of the discussion I ran upstairs, got the book, and brought it to Luther to defend his point. When I handed it to him he kissed me and said, "My little sister knows more about this than a lot of you."

I always valued being around Luther. He always made me feel important and smart. He once gave me a little necklace; it had a blue stone in the center with blue enameled leaves on the side. I was 12 when he gave it to me; I felt somewhat ashamed—good Mormon girls weren't supposed to have jewelry or other flashy things—but it made me feel special. I still treasure it.

Luther went on mission to England in 1912. In the Mormon Church, men are expected to go on a mission for two years to recruit converts. The night before he left, we had a tremendous celebration for him. We sang:

I am a Mormon boy
I might be envied by a king
Because I am a Mormon boy.

I cried for my brother. I knew I would miss him, but I was simply so proud that he was going to another country to spread Mormonism; it was all so wonderful.

But as the months passed, Luther gradually became disillusioned with the church. He had been sent to the mill towns in Liverpool and Blackburn, where he witnessed the despair of exploited laborers. He won converts, but his letters home revealed that he was afraid these people were converting for self-serving economic reasons, not religious or spiritual reasons.

Luther's skepticism about religion and his willingness to question the church gave me a lot of strength. He was a model to me. He refused to accept doctrine without thinking or questioning. When he was on his mission, he noticed how financial issues and working conditions often had more to do with recruitment than spiritual conversion. For many, Mormonism offered a second chance, an opportunity to start over in America. Although I admired and respected my brother's spunk, I didn't begin to question the vision of the world that I had been taught until I was much older. At the time, I accepted what I was taught and chose not to ask too many questions.

After high school I enrolled at BYU and studied to be a teacher. And although I took a broad liberal arts curriculum, I did not learn about the labor movement or the bloody history of the labor struggles in the West. I had never heard of Joe Hill, the radical labor organizer who was executed in Salt Lake City. And, aside from my glimpse of the strike in 1918, I never even encountered any industrial workers—which in Utah meant miners and railroad men—because most of these people lived far from the farm and market society where I lived. I graduated from college before I learned that Black workers were imported to Utah from Tennessee to help break the railroad strike. These Black men were never seen in the community; they were housed and fed in Pullman cars and shipped out as soon as the strike was settled.

My college years were a time of great stress. While I was at BYU my father became very sick. In those days, there were no pensions; after leaving the school system, my father taught seminary for the Mormon Church to help support the family. He was told that he would not lose his salary if someone would cover his classes, so I did. That year, I taught his classes, finished my own senior-level classes at BYU, and developed ulcers and severe stomach problems that have stayed with me all my life.

I worried that I couldn't manage graduating with honors—as everyone in my family had—if I took on the responsibility of teaching my father's classes, too. But I never considered not helping my father. It was a great experience despite the hardship because my father spent time going over the lessons with me. I wasn't really comfortable teaching Mormon philosophy, so he had me teach the history of the church and the history of religion instead. My graduation from BYU in 1927 was my father's last public appearance; he died that summer.

During college I had a serious boyfriend. He was a couple years older than most men in non-Mormon colleges because he had already taken time out to go on his mission. As a returning missionary, he earned the campus title, YDD, Young Doctor of Divinity, which made him a good catch. He wanted to marry me as soon as we finished college. In fact, during a job interview, he told his employer that I was going to be his wife. The life he offered was very tempting, but I knew I wasn't in love with him.

Growing up, I had been taught by the church that on earth my obligation was to marry and bear children. In religious terms, having children would free the spirits from the prelife and give them bodily form so they could start their journey toward the Celestial Kingdom. It didn't all sit right with me.

When I would discuss my religious doubts with my boyfriend, he would tell me to pray more and to accept more on faith. He told me to think of religion as a pocketwatch: "God is the mainspring and we are the cogs turning around him. Each of us has an ability to lead or follow, each doing our part." From his description, I got the clear idea that God saw him as a bigger cog than me.

I also knew that I wasn't ready to marry, even though it would make my mother happy. She told me that I should not put myself ahead of my boyfriend. "It's your duty to help him," she would say. I didn't argue with her, but I didn't get married either.

Instead, I accepted a job teaching physical education and dance at the Branch Agricultural College in Cedar City, Utah. This choice came as quite a blow to my mother because she had convinced the Board of Education for Provo to offer me a job. I didn't want that job; in part because I wanted to establish my personal independence, but also because I was honored to have an opportunity to move directly from college to teaching at the college level.

I also wanted to get away from my ex-boyfriend and away from home. To leave town meant breaking the custom of the old country, where one of the daughters stayed home to take care of her aged mother. As I was the youngest daughter and the only one with no husband, my family assumed that I would stay in Provo. I knew my mother would have depended too much on me now that my father was gone. As things turned out, she moved to Cedar City with me part of the time; her loneliness brought her. I thought I understood her feelings then, but I don't think I really did. But now that my husband, Oliver, is gone, I know exactly how she suffered. I think I'm much more sympathetic to her now; she just needed to be with somebody.

I enjoyed my early years as a teacher, although I did get into some trouble at the Agricultural College. I was teaching dance, and the great Isadora Duncan was then the rage of the dance world, breaking dancers away from rigid steps and stiff clothes in favor of free gestures and more simple dress. One evening I sent my troupe of dancers out to do an outdoor performance draped in loose, gauzy material that clung to their bodies and floated in the wind. Barefoot, the girls danced across the lawn like nymphs.

The next morning, the bishop and the school board called me in to a meeting. "Sit!" they ordered, glaring at me from around a heavy, square table. "Miss Eggertsen, I don't know how to tell you this, but what you've been doing is immoral. Do you realize that you are weakening the moral fiber of our community by having those girls dance without having their bodies properly covered?"

All that man saw was the bodies and legs; he didn't see any of the beauty of the movement. My thought was, "You're just a dirty old man." I nearly collapsed; I was shocked. The only one to defend me was the bishop. I simply promised to be more careful in the future, just so that I could get out of there.

As I look back, I must admit that my attitude may have reflected how naive I was sexually. Though I had a boyfriend in Provo, I did not feel any passion for him. But when I was in Cedar City, I began dating a local boy who was a great basketball player, a good dancer, and very sexy. He awakened a lot of sexual feelings I never had before. He constantly pressed me for more sexual activity, but I refused.

At the end of our relationship he was going on his mission for the church, so I went to Salt Lake City to say goodbye to him. I stayed in the Newhouse Hotel the night before he left, and in the middle of the night he came to my room and knocked on the door, calling for me. He begged me, saying, "Esther, you owe it to me to sleep with me one night before I leave. I need this to remember you." He used all the usual lines, but I didn't respond. The next morning, he was furious with me. I had been sweating with fear all night, but I lied and told him that I must have been sleeping so soundly that I didn't hear him. I know I would have been raped if I had opened the door.

After he left, I began to consider my future—and I knew it was not in Cedar City and not in Provo. Where then? I wanted to continue my education, so like a lot of other young women in my day, I decided to "go East" to graduate school at Columbia University's Teachers College. I wasn't sure exactly what I was looking for, but I thought I might find it in New York.

Chapter 2

Life Beyond the Valley

My awakening began when I arrived in New York City in 1930. Or, more accurately, it began when I met Oliver Arthur Peterson.

Oliver and I met one evening at a lecture at the local YMCA. I saw a notice posted on a bulletin board at Whittier Hall at Columbia about the lecture; I was new on campus and I wanted to make friends, so I decided to attend. I no longer remember what the lecture was about, but I know that it was sponsored by the Fellowship of Reconciliation, an organization that would go on to sponsor lectures by Martin Luther King, Jr., James Farmer, and other heroes of the civil rights movement.

Just as the session was getting started, I noticed Oliver leaning against the fireplace mantle, and I must admit I thought he was very handsome. He had a strong face, wavy brownish hair, and a sturdy build. I made myself approach him during a punch-and-cookie break, and we got to talking. He was a farmboy—the first in his family to make it to college—full of ideas and passions so different from mine.

Oliver asked me if I had seen the view from the roof. He liked to go up to the rooftop to gaze out over the Hudson River, watching the giant shuttle move back and forth across the steel towers that would someday be the George Washington Bridge.

We walked and talked and argued a lot. We disagreed about most things. Oliver was a Depression farmboy; he hated the banks and speculators. He felt that they had ruined the honest and productive lives of many American farmers. Oliver knew firsthand the vicious exploitation of the moneylenders. He remembered how hard his family had to work just to pay the interest on a loan so that his mother could keep the family farm.

Oliver immersed himself in the radical populist politics that sprang from the depleted soil in the Farm Belt. He counted among his heroes the radical socialist Norman Thomas and Robert LaFolette of the Farm Labor Party. My heroes were the Rockefellers and Fords and Mellons, the businessmen who had organized America's industrial might. The Red scares of the postwar period had convinced me that socialists and their kin were out to destroy the comforts of our capitalist society.

At that time I was a strict, conservative Mormon Republican and very anti-union. Though I had graduated from college with honors, I had never appreciated the complexities of the debate between employers and unions. I had never heard about the labor speed-ups on the assembly lines or how workers were expected to work 12-hour days without overtime pay. Oliver taught me these things, then took me to the Rand School to hear impassioned speeches by labor leaders such as Sidney Hillman and David Dubinsky, among others. These union activists were nothing like I had expected: They seemed to be good, bright, reasonable people.

Oliver and I walked up and down the streets in the Bowery and the Lower East Side of Manhattan. There I smelled the stale, rancid odor of poverty for the first time. We talked to people, chatting about prices and produce. I asked the shoppers, "Do you think this melon is ripe?"—anything to get them into a conversation. I told them that I was a student who was concerned about their working conditions. We got to talking about where they lived and worked, and how many people were living in their cramped quarters. My questions weren't asked as part of any class requirement, but they were certainly a critical part of my education. That experience taught me the importance of talking to people directly. If you want to know about a situation, go out and find out for yourself; don't accept all your information secondhand.

Oliver convinced me to read Upton Sinclair's books about the horrors of meatpacking and the human cost of building the railroads and mining coal. Even though Sinclair's books had been bestsellers, I had not read them or taken them seriously before. These muckraking books forced me to admit what a narrow life I had lived. I felt as though I had a big wall around me when I was growing up in Utah. I felt not only protected and sheltered, but restricted and controlled; important information and ideas had been kept from me.

During our debates, I enjoyed the way Oliver would provoke me and keep me on my toes. He forced me to study and to think about social issues so that I could answer him during our discussions. One time we got kicked out of a park at Columbia University because we argued about the business practices of Henry Ford into the early morning hours after the park had closed. I don't know why I didn't worry more about my reputation; good girls weren't supposed to stay out all night, even if they were debating politics with their boyfriends.

I remember that night in the park as the night I fell in love with Oliver. I found it very exciting that he was so much stronger than I; frankly, I was used to men I could push around a bit. Oliver couldn't understand how I could be so smart about certain things and so dumb about the world. But he never diminished me; he always encouraged me to learn more and made me feel that I could make a difference, that I had something to contribute. In every confrontation, I found that Oliver knew more than I did. I spoke from emotion; he spoke from experience and action. These early discussions taught me what it takes to win an argument: facts and conviction.

I also respected Oliver's spiritual side. His mother had wanted him to be a Lutheran minister. When I met him, he was president of the Lutheran Student Association of the United States. He worked in the summers preaching at a Lutheran church on Riverside Drive near Columbia University. We would sit up the night before the Sundays when he would preach and write sermons and discuss what he had to say. In the morning I would meet him in church to hear him speak. The church paid a whopping $25 per lecture, enough to pay for many of his school expenses.

As we got to know one another, Oliver told me about his family. He had grown up in poverty. His mother had wanted him to go to college, and one of his high school teachers recognized his ability and urged him to attend. When Oliver told his teacher that he couldn't afford the tuition, she lent him $400 for his undergraduate studies at the University of North Dakota. Oliver accepted the money and eventually paid it back, though it took years of scrimping and saving.

Despite the financial hardship, Oliver's family history is a most stirring love story. His mother, Astrid Bjorge, came to the United States from Vik, Norway, when she was 17 years old. When she arrived, she was supported by a network of other Norwegians who lived in North Dakota. She soon married Ole Peterson, Oliver's father. They had six children, including one who died in infancy. After spending years in North Dakota, the family moved to Longview, Washington, another town filled with lots of Norwegians, where Ole worked as a clerk at a grocery store. He died of tuberculosis in 1909 at the age of 37.

Widowed, the mother of five, and only 28 years old, Astrid did her best to support the family and to get her children educated. They were poor but proud. Oliver used to say, "We had enough food, but sometimes we skipped a few meals." Astrid took in washing, and she would go out on cross-country skis during the winter months to pick up and return the bundles of laundry.

Oliver's mother accepted her life; she never complained and somehow managed to get by. In fact, she and the children found a lot of joy in the simple things. Oliver told me that one Christmas they didn't have enough money to buy gifts, so the family decided to take what little money they had and buy a single item they could all use. They pooled their money and spent one dollar on a watch, which they hung on the wall where everyone could see it.

Back in Norway, Astrid had had a suitor, Iver Wick. Iver loved Astrid, but she left him behind when she came to America. The two parted with a handshake at the dock, but he did not forget her. Iver went to sea, and when he returned years later he decided to go to America to find her. He asked other Norwegians if they knew where she was, and he eventually tracked her down in Puyallup, Washington.

When Iver reached the appropriate town, he saw a little boy walking along the railroad tracks. That boy was Oliver, who at that time was only about five years old. "Do you know where the Widow Peterson lives?" Iver asked. This wasn't a strange request for the son of a washerwoman. Oliver gave the man directions and didn't think anything of it. But when he arrived home at the end of the day, he found the same man standing in the kitchen, and his mother was weeping. Astrid and Iver were reunited and later married.

Oliver's family moved to a 160-acre farm in North Dakota for a time; then they returned to Washington State where Iver worked as a longshoreman. Iver was injured when a big log fell on him while he was loading a boat. He belonged to the longshoreman's union, which was run by Harry Bridges, an alleged Communist. In those days, there was no worker's compensation; an injury could easily push a family into poverty. The only reason Oliver's family survived after his stepfather's injury was because of the hard-fought rights won by Harry Bridges and the union.

As Oliver told me his story, the importance of unions became much clearer, much more relevant. I think part of my early interest in the concerns of working people reflected my love for Oliver and his family.

Not long after he shared this story with me, Oliver proposed marriage. We were sitting on the steps of an old church in Greenwich Village on New Year's Eve, 1931. He said he loved me and wanted to marry me.

I told him, "With your beliefs, I just can't do it." After all, he was a socialist, he smoked a pipe, he wasn't even a Mormon. I tried to push him. I said, "I can't marry a socialist. You'll have to change."

He said, "I won't change; that would be dishonest. I love you, and I want you, but I can't be something I'm not."

I was dumbfounded. It was the first time I had found a man who was strong enough for me. I couldn't manipulate him, and that made me love him more. I accepted his proposal.

That summer, Oliver came home with me to Utah to meet my family. My mother couldn't have been more disappointed with my choice of husband. He was entirely too radical. He later became a Roosevelt Democrat, which was a little bit easier on my family. Later that same summer, Mother and I drove up to Longview, Washington, to meet Oliver's family. That visit helped my mother accept Oliver because she saw that he came from a good, solid family. I think my mother saw the parallels between her people coming from Denmark and Oliver's people coming from Norway. During that summer, we bridged a lot of the gaps.

Initially it was difficult for me to lose my mother's approval, but it was lovely to see her change as life went on. By the end she was quite proud of me, and she accepted Oliver, too. When she criticized what she considered my radical ideas, I teased her that she had been the one to set me down the wrong path. I reminded her that she actually taught me the first radical song I ever learned. When my mother lived in Denmark as a little girl, she spent time with the workmen in the fields. It was the early days of the socialist movement, and the workers taught her songs, including radical labor songs.

Even at age seven, my mother had a beautiful voice, and one night at a big party, my grandparents asked my mother to sing for the guests. She got up in front of the crowd and began singing a revolutionary labor song. I still remember part of the song as Mother taught it to me: "Rise up you men with the barked hands"—I remember asking what barked meant, and she said it was hands that looked like tree bark from working so hard—"they're digging your graves—revolt." All of my grandparents' friends were shocked, scandalized. By the time I was grown, my mother had a good sense of humor about the entire episode.

Oliver and I were married in 1932 in the Little Church Around the Corner on 29th Street in Manhattan. I confess that I wondered up to the last minute whether I was doing the right thing. My sister

Anne-Marie and another very dear friend served as witnesses. We had planned to have a very small ceremony in New York and a reception back in Utah, but it didn't turn out that way. I didn't hear any noise or commotion when Oliver and I exchanged our vows— I suppose I was just so intent on what we were saying—but when it was over, we turned around and saw that the church was packed. A tourist bus had stopped and crowds of people had slipped into the back of the church.

That summer, Oliver and I went to Europe on a delayed honeymoon. On the trip we brought $1,000—our total savings—and my mother. My parents had always planned to return to Europe to visit their families, but they never did. My mother saw this as a last chance to visit her homeland, and we were pleased to have her along.

The three of us traveled along with some friends who had been invited by the German government. At that time, Hitler was coming into power and the government encouraged visitors who would become sympathetic voices in the United States. We did not officially join the tour group; we simply tagged along at our own expense. Because of the connection, however, we gained access to a number of sightseeing opportunities we probably would not have had on our own.

In retrospect, I can appreciate the significance of some of the unusual things we saw. In particular I remember going into a classroom and seeing a map picturing a number of countries surrounding and pointing guns and bayonets toward Germany. That episode made me see how German propaganda was being used to encourage the German people to band together against the rest of the world. In light of subsequent history, that memory seems quite eerie.

On the trip we went to Denmark and Norway, hoping to find out exactly why our people emigrated to the United States. My mother had left Denmark when she was seven years old, but on this trip when she landed in Vedham, her hometown, she got off the train, looked up and saw the steeple of a church, and knew exactly how to make her way home.

Our stay in Denmark just happened to coincide with a huge funeral for my grandmother's sister, who was the last remaining matriarch in the family. She was the final mistress of the *gärd*, and she had one of the last big Danish funerals, lasting four or five days. As family, we were expected to help with the funeral preparations. Everyone pitched in; I was assigned to work in the kitchen, Oliver worked the fields. According to custom, during the entire celebration everyone who came to the door had to be fed. Little kids would come to the door again and again, just to collect another cookie or cake. When the time came for the burial, Theo Kragh, my mother's sister's husband, a big, sinewy farmer, tied the flowers to the casket with wire as though he were baling hay. It made me think of his barked hands. He then led the funeral processional.

In Norway, we arrived in Oliver's mother's home town of Vik at about 4:00AM. We arrived by mail boat, then stumbled along a little path leading to a small town. It was dark and we were in the middle of nowhere; I didn't want to see that boat pull away from shore. We wandered up the path, then saw smoke coming out from a single building in the village. Oliver knocked on the door and a baker answered. He was busy baking bread for the day, but he invited us in. Oliver could speak a little Norwegian, and more words came back to him as he spoke. He told the man he was the son of Astrid. The baker smiled and said again and again, *"Hon var so pen"*—she was so beautiful.

Oliver was thrilled to find someone who knew his mother as a girl. Word traveled that Astrid's son had returned, and we were welcomed into houses throughout the village. The reception exceeded all our expectations. The baker took us into his living room, which was used only for special occasions. We were honored guests. We saw evergreen boughs strung over the doorways of some of the houses. One woman explained that the green marked special occasions, usually weddings, births, and funerals. She said that if she had known we were coming, she would have put greens up for us because it was a special day; Astrid's son had returned.

After Oliver and I married we lived in Boston, where Oliver studied at Harvard and taught for the Affiliated School for Workers.

I taught physical education at Winsor School for Girls, an aristocratic girls' college-prep school. Before I accepted the job, I had been warned that the school had an upper-class reputation. One of the sayings about the area was—
Here's to the land of Boston
The home of beans and the cod
Where Lowells speak only to Cabots,
And Cabots speak only to God.

It was old society, old money. A rumor circulated that a woman who found out her daughter was pregnant had called the school, requesting that if the baby were a girl that a spot be reserved for her at Winsor.

The school was beautiful, with big red brick buildings, an indoor swimming pool, tennis courts, and a big hockey field. When I arrived, Miss Winsor was still alive; she founded the school because she recognized the need for girls to get a good education, just as the boys got at Phillips-Exeter and Groton. The philosophy of the school was something I supported—equal educational opportunities for girls and boys—but some of the girls were not yet sufficiently mature to appreciate all their advantages. Many of them considered privilege a birthright.

I wasn't always comfortable there. I came from a more modest background, not from the upper crust. My first trouble surfaced when I tried to modernize the athletic program. I wanted all the girls to learn athletic skills and to take part in sports and tennis and swimming. These programs were available on the side for girls who wanted to stay after school, but the actual gym classes were filled with marching and dumbbell swinging.

I had difficulty making my point. First, I was an outsider. I was from Utah; I didn't speak with a Boston accent. And, more important, no one wanted change. When I began suggesting improvements in the program, I was told, "Our forebears have all marched. We see no need for change."

The girls also wore heavy bloomers with white shirts. I wanted to throw away the bloomers in favor of colorful gym suits, a different color for each class. That way, out on the fields, it would be easy to spot the different teams. I talked to the art teacher and we picked out the colors. I won that battle the first year. It made a lot of sense.

When I first arrived, many of the girls didn't like me one bit. They eventually came around—they gave me quite a send-off six years later—but in the beginning it was hell. The girls called me Miss Eggie of the Department of Peristalsis and Perspiration. I had the most trouble with one group, Class 6, girls who were 13 or 14 years old. On some days I would go to class and the girls would ignore me. They decided they wanted me out; they had favored the woman who taught before I arrived. She had kept her favorite girls on all the sports teams, but I was determined to let everyone play, not just the select group. The school had an excellent field hockey team, and I was expected to wink at the best players and design the programs around them, leaving the other girls with the same, boring, unchallenging program they had been dragging through for years. I thought it was time for a change.

I tried to teach tap dancing. It was quite the craze, and I was good at it. A lot of the girls weren't interested in the sports program, but I thought they might want to try dance. Some of the parents were enraged: "You mean we're paying someone to teach our children tap dancing?" We took the seats out of the assembly hall so that we could dance in a large room. Miss Catherine Lord, the director of the school, was wonderful about it. She understood what I was trying to do; she also wanted the girls to get more involved.

The girls expressed their displeasure by trying to make me feel socially inferior. The teachers had to preside over the tables at the daily luncheons. I admit that before I went to Winsor I had never learned how to use a fish fork, nor had I attended meals that required the use of a fingerbowl, but I knew that those things didn't really matter.

One day I asked the girls to pass the tomatoes. They ignored me. I asked again, and one of the girls said, "Oh, you mean the toe-mah-toes."

"I mean the toe-may-toes. Pass them," I said sternly. Those girls would do anything to humiliate me and to get me to leave. One girl actually put her feelings into words: "You're not one of us; you better get out." She had no idea how stubborn I could be. The more they tried to get me out, the more determined I was to stay. I vowed not to leave.

My sister Anne-Marie also taught at Winsor, and she tried desperately to fit in. She had started at Winsor before I arrived; in fact, she told the headmistress about me. Anne-Marie was uncomfortable admitting she was a Mormon from Utah. She was insecure about her social standing, a feeling I well understood as the girls so often went out of their way to make newcomers feel like outsiders. Anne-Marie's husband, Briant, was in medical school at Harvard, and he was from Idaho. When asked where she was from, she said that she and her husband were from Idaho.

I saw no need to apologize for who I was. When I met people, I told them I was from Utah. People were confused that I was from Utah and Anne-Marie was from Idaho. I didn't blow the whistle; after all, her husband was from Idaho and she had lived there part of the time.

Anne-Marie really wanted to belong. We never had social teas in Utah; of course, Mormons weren't supposed to drink tea in the first place. At Winsor there were faculty teas in the afternoon. When Anne-Marie went to her first tea, someone asked, "Would you like lemon in your tea?"

She said, "Oh yes, please."

Then someone else said, "Would you like cream?"

And again she said, "Oh yes, please."

Of course, the cream instantly curdled. The woman serving stared at her, and Anne-Marie said, "Oh, this is how we drink tea back home."

As I look back, I am much more sympathetic to Anne-Marie's need to fit in. And I am much more sympathetic to the girls' resistance to rapid change. I was young, and I now see that I wanted to move the school into the modern world too fast. I didn't appreciate the importance of taking things one step at a time. Change requires patience, and a lot of little steps.

I usually got along quite well with the directors of the school, but one exception really stands out—my big goof-up with the May

Day celebration. Every year, the girls would set up big maypoles and dance around them. One year, I set up six poles, one for each class. They were 12 or 14 feet tall, with different colored streamers, representing the different classes. There were streamers on each pole, and the girls would waltz around the poles, weaving in and out, braiding the ribbons together.

Miss Lord, the director of the school, had a close friend visiting from England, so I decided to make the spring celebration extra special by having the girls dance in old-fashioned costumes of long, colorful skirts, instead of their conventional dress.

The following morning, Miss Lord called me into her office and chided me for breaking the tradition of the maypole dancing. It seems that Miss Lord's friend had been a British traditionalist, and that the addition of the costumes and flourishes was considered inappropriate. In Great Britain, the girls wore simple blouses and skirts. After that we always did the maypole dancing the old-fashioned way as the school tradition decreed. That taught me another lesson: Understand and appreciate a group's traditions before trying to make a change. Everything has a history, even maypole dancing.

During our early years as a married couple, Oliver and I spent our weeks working in Massachusetts and our weekends skiing and camping and hiking in Vermont. In 1935 we put $50 down and bought a 187-acre farm in Townshend, Vermont, near Brattleboro; we paid a total of $1,200. The deed actually says, "200 acres, more or less." At the time, we imagined setting up a summer retreat and school for working people. The school never materialized, but for nearly 60 years it has been a true family homestead. When we bought the farm we had no idea that it would become such a stable and important part of our lives. Going to Vermont means going home; it's the one thing in our lives that seems to be a constant.

The farm wasn't much to speak of when we bought it. It was quite run down, with broken front steps and boarded windows. One window had a tin can with a geranium in it. A poor family lived in the house. We gave them plenty of time to find a new home in Brattleboro, and in the meantime we spent our weekends camping by the brook. Oliver had made a nest of boughs and branches at a campsite, but we were eager to settle into our new home.

When we arrived on the appointed date with our things ready to move in, the family was still there. Oliver asked, "Why are you still here?"

"We're not ready yet," came the reply.

"Why aren't you getting your things together now?" Oliver asked.

"Well, we ain't got our sittin' done yet." That became a family phrase whenever there was work to be done, but little enthusiasm to get it done: I ain't got my sittin' done yet. We still use the expression.

Oliver and I loved the farm and all the potential it represented. My mother didn't see things that way. One weekend we brought her to the farm, and my entire past descended on me. We walked across some grass and Oliver and I explained how we were going to plant a garden and my mother looked at me with tears in her eyes.

"Esther, you don't need to do this," she said. "This is why we left the old country." She thought that Oliver was dragging me down rather than pushing me forward; she thought we were going to become slaves to the land. My mother was very proud of her past, of having been the first woman in the family to graduate from college, to have a chance to make something of her life. I tried to explain that we loved the place and that we were making a choice.

We went back to the house and I made a pot of coffee. We sat on the porch and looked out at the long, satisfying views of the rolling hills. She said, "This is a beautiful place." I think she understood how right it all felt. I appreciated her concern; she was afraid we would become homesteaders. At that time, jobs were hard to come by, and everyone was struggling. She never understood why we didn't want comforts like a telephone and electricity. (The place still doesn't have electricity, although we did install a phone in the 1970s when Oliver was sick.) We lived by the motto, If you're cold, chop wood. If you're thirsty, haul water.

In the Mormon Church, we were always raised to do something for other people. When I arrived in Boston, almost by habit, I found a meeting of the Young Ladies Mutual Improvement Association, the youth league of the Mormon Church. Oliver said, "Oh Esther, do something different." Oliver was always challenging me to push myself and try new experiences.

Instead of doing community work through the church, I volunteered at the local Young Women's Christian Association (YWCA). Again, my Utah friends were appalled. I was invited to a meeting of the Mormon Relief Society in Boston, and several of the women asked me to explain what I was doing. Afterward, one of the women told Anne-Marie that it was a "tragic waste" that I was involved with working-class issues. They thought I was a radical; I was going to the dogs.

At the Y, I was assigned to the industrial department. On Thursday nights, I taught current events in a class I called "What's Happening in the World Today." We took the local newspaper, *The Boston Transcript* (it's gone now), and we read and discussed the news. The students were working girls: factory workers, maids, and domestic workers. Most of the garment workers were Italian; the domestics were Irish. So many of the girls came from different countries and had different ideas about the world. After our discussions, we did some gymnastics and dancing—tap dancing, folk dancing, the Virginia Reel.

I didn't want to do the Lady Bountiful stuff; I just wanted to do my part to enrich the lives of these girls. I began to really feel the contrast between the wealth of the girls I taught at Winsor during the day and the poverty of the working girls I taught at the Y at night. I found the working girls so much more warm and loving, so much more real, than most of the girls at Winsor. Some of the domestic workers were actually employed by the families of the girls at Winsor.

Not surprisingly, I found the working girls much more aware of how the real world worked. At times I actually felt sorry for some of the Winsor girls. When one of the Winsor girls started menstruating, she came crying to me, begging for help. She thought she had internal bleeding. No one had told her about the changes taking place in her body. She had a governess and a maid, she had tea with her mother almost every day, but no one ever really talked to her about what she needed to know. So many of these girls had economic advantages, but they were emotionally neglected.

Through my work at the Y, I became quite concerned about the racial situation. There were no Blacks in my classes, no Blacks at the Y. When I inquired, I was told that the Blacks could go to another Y across town. But our Y had a swimming pool and nicer facilities. I argued that at a minimum we should open the pool to the Blacks, since they couldn't swim otherwise.

"We can't do that," I was told. When I pressed the issue, someone scolded, "It just isn't done."

I was concerned. I had a meeting with some of the members of the Industrial Committee. I said, "Let's get out our statement of purpose. What do we believe in?"

Of course, the statement of purpose declared support for equality and justice. I said, "If we believe that, how can we discriminate?"

"It's custom and practice," I was told. I always remembered that phrase, a very empty argument for discrimination.

"Then let's strike out this passage where it says we believe in equality. Clearly, we don't believe that."

The point was clear. It didn't happen right away, but eventually the Y was integrated, and I like to think my experience there helped.

I've used that what-do-we-believe method several times to win arguments. I've had some wonderful fights with it. When you confront people with the difference between what they say and what they do, they must change one or the other.

To be honest, I wasn't always so confident or sure of what I believed. I was learning a lot from the girls I was teaching at the Y. My real education came in the fall when I arrived in class and more than half the girls were missing. I asked where the other girls were and I was told they were on strike. A strike? Of course, I knew much more about labor issues and workers' rights than I had just a few years before, but part of me still felt that a strike was something terrible, with people walking the picket lines with bombs in their pockets. Until that point, most of my discussions and debates over labor were intellectual exercises; this time, I knew the people on the picket line.

Chapter 3

Bread and Roses

My heart pounded as I walked up the rickety steps. This was my first venture into the slums of Cambridge, although I had heard about them from my brother-in-law Briant, who went into the slums to help deliver babies. Briant had told me about the poverty—and the strength—of the families living there, but still I thought to myself, "What am I getting into?" I couldn't be sure, but I had to find out. I knew something was wrong, and I kept thinking about the girls from the garment factories who lived there and who had walked out on strike. Those girls were so young, so harmless, and yet so strong. They had refused to accept a situation that they knew was unfair. That's what brought me up those steps.

I went there hoping to visit one of the girls in my class at the Y who was a bit older and more mature than the other girls; I think her name was Eileen. She was only about 16 years old, but she was a leader, both in class and among the other workers. Her voice even rose above the others when we sang in class. I needed to get her to explain the situation. I knew where I could find her because she once had given me her address and invited me to visit her.

I knocked on the door and Eileen answered. Inside, five children and their mother sat around a table; the room was illuminated by a single, naked lightbulb hanging from the ceiling. Eileen invited me inside and introduced me to her family.

The children looked up, then went right on with their work. Even the youngest child—no more than three years old—worked;

he sat in a high chair counting out bobby pins into piles of 10. I'll never forget that sight because the bobby pins were the same brand I used to buy. The pins were slipped onto a card that said, "Count 'em, 10, count 'em." Some of the kids divided the pins into piles; others put them on the cards. The older kids were putting strings through tags that hung on the clothes sold at Filene's, a big Boston department store. For the first time, I really knew what industrial homework and child labor were about. It was still a shock to see such problems firsthand.

I asked Eileen why she had missed class. She explained that she and many of the other girls in class were out on strike. They worked in a factory in south Boston making cotton wrap housedresses, known as Hoover dresses. The girls were paid $1.32 per dozen dresses, which worked out to about 10¢ per hour. I believe the dresses then sold in department stores for about $3 or $4 each.

The girls felt frustrated because their employer had changed the design of the pocket on the dresses from a square to a heart. "A square is easy to sew, but have you ever tried to sew around the curves of a heart?" asked Eileen. The girls wanted to be paid $1.50 per dozen dresses. If they didn't get a raise, they would make less money for more work. The boss refused any wage increase, so about half the workers—30 or 40 girls—walked out in what soon became known as The Heartbreaker Strike.

Such a bold step wasn't taken lightly; for many of the girls, not working meant not eating. A lot of the girls came from large families, which they had to help support. I believe Eileen's father was a rubber worker, but he didn't make enough money to support his wife and children. In Eileen's family and in many others, everyone needed to contribute to make ends meet.

By the time I left Eileen's house, I knew that I supported her struggle; I was on her side. I felt angry about the girls' exploitation and frustrated that they could be taken advantage of so easily. These girls had no power, no rights—and now they had no jobs.

The following morning, I stood side by side with the girls on the picket line. A small group of girls stood in front of the building, trying to stop the workers who did not join the strike from going in.

It was painful for me to watch the girls turn against one another. The day before, the strikers and strikebreakers had worked next to one another; today they were enemies. Tensions grew when the strikers learned that the boss had given the girls who stayed at work a little more money.

Police on horses showed up and pushed the strikers back, reminding me of the horses I saw at the railroad strike of 1918 when I was a girl—only this time I was on the workers' side of the picket line. I wore my old blue coat and I wasn't too much older than the other girls, so I was treated as though I were a striker and pushed back and frightened with the others.

Organizers from the International Ladies Garment Workers Union (ILGWU) showed up and helped support the strike, even though the girls had not yet joined a union. By the end of the day, however, the girls were singing, "The Union Makes Us Strong"— and I was singing along with them.

That first day I was scared to death that I'd be arrested; I had to be at school at 8:30. I marched the line, singing and chanting as the girls arrived at work, then I rushed off, changed clothes, and hurried to school before the first bell.

I didn't want to compromise my job at Winsor School by participating in this untraditional activity, so I went to Catherine Lord, the director of the school, and said, "Miss Lord, I must tell you about what I'm doing, but I want you to know that I feel very strongly about it." I explained to her about my volunteer work at the YWCA and how I had learned about the strike. I told her that I wanted both to keep my job and to help these women.

After a long discussion, she concluded, "If it doesn't interfere with the quality of your teaching, what you do in your own time is your own affair." I so admired her courage. She was a great woman. If necessary, she was willing to challenge the other school authorities to let me take a stand. She stood to lose a lot more than I did from this situation, which could easily be misunderstood as radical and inappropriate. From that day forward, I have considered her to be one of my heroines.

I returned to the picket line on the second day of the strike, but I wore my best clothes—complete with a fur and high heels—and I was treated like royalty. I called some of the women I knew who were on the board at the YWCA and members of the Women's Trade Union League and they joined me; I think we called ourselves the Citizen's Committee of Concerned Women. I didn't know these women well, but I knew they shared my concern for the struggles of the strikers. Our presence on the picket line gave the strike respectability, and it provided the girls with an additional measure of protection.

In a few weeks the girls had officially formed a local of the ILGWU; they were back on the job, with a raise—and I had become a trade unionist. I was changed forever by the experience of seeing firsthand how unions empowered workers. Alone, the girls were voiceless; together, they were a force to be reckoned with.

This link between collective bargaining and women's empowerment was very exciting to me. I became more involved with the National Women's Trade Union League in Boston, a group that was concerned with the rights and the working conditions of women in industry. The group would support certain strikes by joining the workers on the picket line and by offering financial support. Almost all the members were women, which explains why there was a lot of concern about women and women's problems. At that time I was more comfortable working with organizations run by women than those run by men. In the men's organizations, I spent most of my time on the outside, listening. In the women's groups I could really take part.

Through the Women's Trade Union League, I met Bob Watt, president of the American Federation of Labor in Boston. He took me to a sit-down strike at a textile mill in New Bedford, Massachusetts. The workers were striking over wages and their right to form a union. I was really just a kid in my 20s, volunteering to help out. Everything was new to me. The image that stays with me is of standing in a red brick courtyard at night, looking up at the face of a multistory factory with dozens of workers leaning out the windows. They were holding on to their jobs with all they had.

I helped out by leading the singing, starting with "Solidarity Forever," the anthem of the American Labor Movement (sung to the tune "Glory, Glory, Hallelujah"):

> When the union's inspiration through the workers' blood shall run
> There can be no power greater anywhere beneath the sun
> Yet what force on earth is weaker than the feeble strength of one
> But the union makes us strong.

I knew the songs kept the workers' spirits up and made them feel that there were many on their side. It was all spontaneous; there was nothing deliberate about it. The supporters in the courtyard sang and cheered the strikers on.

Because it was a sit-down strike, the workers refused to leave the building; they guarded their machines to protect their jobs. If they walked out, strikebreakers would file in and take their places. The sit-down strike was their most effective way of holding on to their jobs. These sit-down strikes were so effective that in 1937 and afterward a number of states considered legislation to outlaw them.

Another song we sang celebrated the strength of the sit-down strike:

> When they tie the can to a union man,
> Sit down! Sit down!
> When they give him the sack, they'll take him back,
> Sit down! Sit down!
> Sit down, just take a seat,
> Sit down and rest your feet
> Sit down you've got 'em beat
> Sit down! Sit down!
> When the boss won't talk, don't take a walk
> Sit down! Sit down!
> When the boss sees that, he'll want to chat.
> Sit down! Sit down!

I so loved the lyrics, the spirit, the passion of these songs.

The more involved I became in union issues, the more I wanted to learn about them. I continued to support various strikers as a volunteer. Once when working at a strike at a textile mill in Lawrence, Massachusetts, not long after the sit-down strike, I saw my first "shape-up." I went to a room where workers gathered to seek employment; the bosses then entered, looked them over, and picked from the crowd those who could work. Most shape-ups involved longshoremen, but this was a shape-up for the textile workers.

I heard a man say, "How many of you will work for $1 an hour?"

Of course, all the unemployed workers put their hands up; that was a good wage.

Then he said, "How many will work for 75¢?"

Most of the hands stayed up. Eventually, he worked his way down to 25¢ an hour and got all the workers he needed.

I asked one of the workers why he accepted the low wage and he said, "My kids are hungry." His only alternative was no work—and no pay.

Again, this reinforced in my mind the need for workers, especially women workers, to recognize their strength through their numbers. The men were treated badly, but the women were treated worse.

At this time, my economic philosophy was beginning to take shape: There was something wrong with an economic system that depended on workers' labor but gave workers little or no say about their working conditions. I became a member of the National Consumers League for Fair Labor Standards, which remains the oldest national consumer organization in the nation's history. I supported the group's philosophy that consumers could help shape the economy and improve the conditions of workers through their purchases.

One of the league's major projects was a white-label campaign: The official Consumers League White Label would be sewn only into garments manufactured under fair working conditions. The label indicated to shoppers which products they could buy with a clear conscience. I began to understand that the economy was really a three-legged stool—with workers, producers, and consumers each taking part.

Although I was just getting started in the consumer movement, I did make some speeches for the Consumers League. We repeatedly used the phrase, "using our purchasing power to help guide social policy." None of the women was trained in public speaking; we just spoke from the heart. I've always felt that if you have something important to say, you will have no trouble saying it. Public speaking didn't make me nervous because as a member of the Mormon Church, I had spoken in Sunday school and testimony meetings from an early age. I had addressed large crowds before, but the Consumers League speeches were my first about issues involving social policy.

My work with the labor unions made me very sensitive to issues involving working women, and I was particularly responsive to a message I heard from Bryn Mawr College's Hilda "Jane" Worthington Smith. During a Wednesday assembly at Winsor School, Smith spoke about the "left-out women," working women who did not get a chance to get a good education because they had to work.

During the speech, Smith told the girls at Winsor about how M. Carey Thomas, president of Bryn Mawr College, got the inspiration in 1920, while sitting on a golden hilltop in the Sahara Desert, to establish a workers' school. She envisioned a school that included workers from the United States and from throughout the world. Thomas considered it wasteful that college campuses sat dormant throughout the summer, while so many working women needed an education. Thomas developed a summer school for women workers, modeling the program after a similar school in England. She wanted to provide the girls with a solid liberal education, as well as skills in clear thinking. In turn, she wanted the workers to feel less isolated, less alone.

The school opened in June 1921 with 81 students. In the early years, the girls studied science—everything from astronomy to zoology—and English, as well as economics and political history. Over time, English and economics became the core curriculum.

Working women and girls received scholarships raised by Bryn Mawr alumnae. The only requirements for enrollment were that the girls had to have earned their own living for three years, have a sixth-grade education, and be able to read and write English.

I was touched when Jane asked the privileged girls at Winsor to think about how they might get by if they had to earn their own living for three years. I had so often thought of the differences between the girls I taught at the Y and the girls I taught at Winsor. Many of them were the same age, but the working girls understood responsibility; they were mature, focused, and appreciative. At Winsor I knew that teachers had to try to make learning attractive to students; with the working girls, all that was needed was to provide the material and ideas because the girls were eager to learn.

Captivated by Smith's speech, I knew I wanted to be a part of the summer school. After assembly, I stood at the entrance to the assembly hall, waiting for Smith to come out. I wore my gym bloomers with a skirt wrapped around for decency; I felt self-conscious of my dress, but I considered it more important to speak my mind. I approached Smith on her way out and told her that I believed in what she was doing and that I wanted to work with her.

She gave me a summer job as recreation director, teaching sports and handling the theater, music, dance, and all the extracurricular programs, a jack-of-all-trades really. In all, about 70 students attended the school each summer; most were first-generation immigrants, but some came from Czechoslovakia, Holland, Germany, Puerto Rico, England, and Sweden.

The six summers I spent at the Bryn Mawr Summer School for Women Workers in Industry provided me with the best education on workers' issues that I could have experienced. In the mornings, I attended the regular economics and English classes. The girls were divided into groups, depending on what industry they represented. Every group included workers from all the basic types of industries; in a sense, each group represented an economic microcosm of the world. The workers in each group offered such rich life experiences that the class basically involved learning from one another. Textbooks were secondary; the course structure came from experience.

The discussions often seemed simple and revolutionary at the same time. I'll never forget one discussion about the definitions of labor and worth. I found it exciting to watch a laundry worker make the connection that she was selling her labor as a commodity. Her employer made her feel that she was nobody and contributed nothing of real value because she didn't make a final product. But during the discussion she realized that she had something to sell— her labor. She's not selling a shirt; she's selling herself and her skills. This concept was especially important for working women because so many of them were not accustomed to having anyone put any economic value on the work they did, either at home or on the job.

I had taken economics in college, but until I witnessed the dialogue between those working women, I never really understood the importance of labor as a commodity. I credit the professors with allowing the discussion to be very human, very down to earth. The professors who taught the classes came from some of the best universities in the United States, including Colston Warne of Amherst (who went on to become president of Consumers Union and publisher of *Consumer Reports*); Earl Cummins, head of the economics department at Union College; and Helen Lockwood, a professor at Vassar College, among others.

The professors did such a fine job of teaching the girls about the labor movement that the girls began to see their lives in new ways. One student who was very special to me, Anne E. Butler, a Black laundry worker, became a good friend. We spent hours reading and writing poetry together. Over the course of the summer, she gained a better understanding of the labor movement and her role in it, and this shift showed up in her poetry:

A steaming cup of black coffee in a delicate china cup,
She handed me.
"Sugar, Anne?"
"Yes," I replied.
"Just a bit, to take the bitterness off."
I paused abruptly. My cup poised in midair, I thought
Grimly, those big money men are always offering us a bit
Of sweet to take the bitterness out of the scummy liquid

They're handing us. And most of us poor gullible fools
Just gulp it right down and say contented,
"Humm, it's not so bad now."

That poem crystallized her understanding of the labor movement. A deep regret I have is that I lost touch with her sometime after we both left the summer school.

As recreation director at the summer school, one of my favorite activities involved staging our so-called "Saturday Night Specials." We put on performances based on current events and what the students were studying in class. One of the best performances involved the packing of the Supreme Court. The skit was titled "Packing, Packing, Packing, or the Supreme Court at Bay"; it was presented by a group of the students ("with some packing"). This session took place at the time that President Roosevelt was trying to pack the court by raising the number of justices who supported his New Deal efforts. We took the history of the Supreme Court and outlined some of the key decisions in verse, then chanted the lyrics to the tune of "Jingle Bells." We made floodlights out of tomato cans. None of the scripts was carefully written; we improvised as we went along. Of course, we rehearsed a bit and talked about what we should include, but there were no written lines, except the song lyrics. The performances helped the students really see the history and understand the issues. It was education and recreation in one.

Another Saturday night play helped spark a racial awakening in me. Unfortunately, I had been taught by the Mormon culture that African-Americans were Black because they were cursed in heaven for having made a wrong religious decision. As a child, I thought that people sat on a fence and that they would fall one way or another and become Black or White, depending on whether they made the right or wrong decision. Of course, by the time I was an adult, I understood and appreciated—at least intellectually—racial differences, but my exposure to Black people had been minimal. Growing up, the only Black person I knew was the cook at the Roberts Hotel in Provo.

One Saturday night we put on a play titled, "America, You Called Us to Your Shores," which showed why our different nationalities came to the United States. Groups representing different nationalities met separately, then took turns performing their segments. I felt proud when the Danish girls took the stage and talked about coming to America in search of religious freedom. I thought of my grandparents, crossing the Atlantic, following the Mormon missionaries. It set me in history.

Then a group of African-American students walked on stage dressed in sack-cloth. They stood tall, stared into the audience and said, "We did not ask to come. We did not want to come. We were captured and brought as slaves."

They said nothing more. The audience was silent. Those few minutes made real my understanding of Black history. What was once theoretical became human. Those three lines struck me in a way that made the racial issue real to me.

But that's not to say my transformation was immediate or complete. One day I was urging the girls to hurry up and get down to the field. I said, "The last one there's a nigger-baby." I didn't mean to be offensive; to me, it was the same thing as saying, "Last one there's a rotten egg." I said it without thinking; I just used a phrase that I heard as a child. I didn't understand that nigger was derogatory; at home I often heard the word, and back in Salt Lake City I heard the cheap seats up in the balcony at the movies referred to as the seats up in "nigger heaven." Indeed, the Mormon Church institutionalized racial prejudice: Until 1978 it excluded "Blacks of African lineage" from the essential rites of the temple ritual and it denied Black men the prerogative of the priesthood. As late as 1969, the church declared, "Negroes [are] not yet to receive the priesthood, for reasons which we believe are known to God, but which He has not made fully known to man."

My ignorance did not excuse my insensitivity. After making the remark, the girls in my class froze and stared back at me. I said it to all the students, both Black and White.

"What's the matter? What did I do?"

The girls said that they were insulted, that I shouldn't talk to them that way. I saw the pain in their faces. I urged them to sit down and talk it out. I wanted to get it all out in the open, put it on the table. The girls told me how they were offended; I explained that I hadn't meant any harm. I never used the word again. I was proud of the girls for standing up and saying what they thought; remember, the civil rights movement was 30 years away.

Over the years, the summer school developed a radical reputation. The end of the line for the school came after a strike at Seabrook Farms Branch of Bridgeton, New Jersey, in the spring and summer of 1934. Seabrook was a huge farm that produced vegetables for canning. A group of teachers from the summer school had learned that the workers had gone on strike to raise their wages to 30¢ an hour for men and 25¢ an hour for women. Wages for some workers had been as low as 5¢ an hour. They also wanted the boss to recognize their union, the Agricultural Workers Industrial Union, Seabrook Farms Branch, and to rehire Jerry Brown, a local activist who had been fired for his involvement with the union.

I decided to join several other summer school teachers who were driving down to witness the strike. We went on the weekend and, it is important to note, we were acting as individuals, not representatives of the school. What we saw will stay with me forever. The Seabrook workers lived in shacks. A trench—an open sewer—ran through the area where the children played. There was violence; tear gas was thrown into workers' homes, even though babies and children were inside.

The press showed up for the strike and reported that teachers from Bryn Mawr Summer School had attended. We knew that the Bryn Mawr Board of Directors considered teacher involvement in the strike radical and inappropriate. We had been hired to be teachers, not activists. Those opposed to the strike claimed that it was Communist-inspired. I learned later that the members of the Communist Party had supported the strike, but that didn't minimize the importance of the issues the workers were fighting for.

It wasn't just the Seabrook strike that caused problems. Some people were upset and claimed that Socialists and Communists wanted to take over the school and indoctrinate the workers with their philosophy. But that was one of the great characteristics of

Hilda Worthington Smith: she said there was room for the Communists and the Socialists, as well as for people who did not agree with them. She stressed that the democratic process was strong enough to include differences of opinion.

In fact, the summer school students studied Marxism—as well as capitalism—as an important social and political movement. The Marxism class actually started because a student was found to be holding private meetings of a Marxist study group. When the school officials found out about the meetings, rather than expel the girls, they agreed to offer a course. In 1934 the summer school administrators hired an academic Marxist to teach a course on Marxism openly. The purpose of the school was to educate, not to inculcate. In the end, Hilda Smith paid a price for her tolerance: Her home was marked with a burning cross and she was investigated by the Martin Dies Committee on Un-American Activites.

Tensions grew too strong after the Seabrook strike. There was an outcry from the Bryn Mawr Board of Directors; the school was not allowed back on campus the following year. I didn't mind being called a radical because I was secure in my beliefs, but I did regret that the school had to move to Mount Ivy in New Jersey in 1935. It stayed in New Jersey for only one summer, then became the Hudson Shore Labor School at Jane Smith's home in West Park, New York, from 1936 to 1938, when it disbanded. During the years it was in operation, the school brought together a total of nearly 1,600 workers from factories, mills, and sweatshops and provided them with a basic education in the humanities. Many of the graduates later became leaders in the labor movement.

My connections at Bryn Mawr eventually led to my first formal experience as a union organizer for the American Federation of Teachers (AFT), a new trade union. At summer school I had become acquainted with the economics department people at Harvard: Ray Walsh, Alan Sweezy, and Bob Lamb. The group tutored students at Harvard and set aside their tutoring money in a fund. They asked me to begin to organize teachers in New England, using this tutoring fund to finance my efforts. I didn't really have to think about the decision; all my experiences had been leading to this point. I left Winsor to take that job. Oliver delighted in my formal move into the labor movement.

By that point I firmly believed in unions as the best way to improve working conditions, and I wanted to organize my own profession, teaching. AFT was an early, left-wing labor group for teachers. During my years with the AFT I organized three New England locals.

First I went to Lawrence, Massachusetts. I had heard that things were bubbling and that it would be a good place to get a teachers' union going. I arrived in town and took a taxi from the train station; I asked the taxi driver about teachers in the area and he mentioned that there was a big teachers meeting that night.

If I had known there was going to be a meeting, I might have tried to blend in, but that day I was very conspicuous in a red suit and hat. I entered a big hall and sat down and began talking to the teachers sitting next to me. They asked me what school I was from; I said I was from out of town, then used whatever charm I had to get them to talk to me.

When the meeting started, someone said, "If there are any people here who should not be here, they should leave now."

I knew the reference was to me, but I thought to myself, "I have every right to be here. I am a teacher, and I believe in what they are doing." I justified my actions within myself, then stayed seated, my heart pounding. I didn't want to offend anyone, but I needed to find out what their complaints were.

During the meeting, I found out that the teachers had genuine grievances: low wages, long hours, and classes crowded with more than 40 students. One teacher said, "We're more like circus trainers than teachers."

The minute the meeting was over, I went over to the Central Labor Union and told them what I had done. Some of the people there knew Frances Masterson, the president of the teachers' group (it wasn't a union at the time). Frances and her sister came over to the Central Labor Union to talk to me; they were furious. They said they had graciously tried to ask me to leave the meeting, but I wouldn't go. I told them that I was a teacher, so I stayed, but because I wasn't an actual member of the group, I didn't speak. After considerable discussion, they were more understanding and willing to accept my help. After all, we were both on the same side. The final result was a new branch of the AFT.

I then went to Springfield, Massachusetts, to try to set up another local, but that was tougher. I arrived in town with a couple of names of teachers who were sympathetic to the union cause. I called them together to meet in my hotel. I had reserved a room with a sitting room off to the side. I saw a man waiting in the sitting room. After the meeting, I found out that he was a reporter with *The Springfield Union*, the local newspaper. He had been eavesdropping throughout the meeting.

After the meeting I went down to the newspaper to speak to the reporter because he did not interview me for his story. I didn't want the paper to undermine my efforts by printing an article that would discourage the teachers from joining the union. I urged the reporter to delay the story, or at least to interview me so that he could tell both sides of the story, but he wanted nothing to do with me.

When I got back to the hotel that night I had a call from Val Burati, another reporter at the paper who had overheard my conversation with his colleague. Burati told me that the first reporter will write what he's told to write. Val then told me whom to talk to and whom to see; he was my unofficial advisor for the whole campaign.

The next day on the front page of the paper was an article describing our efforts to organize a teachers' union. After reading it, I went right to the superintendent of schools to talk to him. I didn't mind confronting him; unlike the teachers in the area, I didn't depend on him for my paycheck. Because my father had been superintendent of schools in Provo, Utah, and I had received a master's degree from Teachers' College at Columbia University, I felt that I was someone he had to listen to. The superintendent had just written a book on teacher representation, and he was very nervous. The last thing he wanted was a teachers' union. We argued a bit, but ultimately it would be up to the teachers themselves to organize.

During the campaign I had a lot of support from the telephone operators at the hotel where I was staying. If someone called who was against the union, they would say I wasn't there and take a message. Then they would brief me on who was with the union movement and who was against it. I had a network of helpers. The working people were wonderful; they understood the importance of the unions. It took a lot of work, but we eventually got a union there.

We also organized in Bennington, Vermont; and we already had a local in Lowell, Massachusetts, so by the time I left the AFT we had a unit of four good New England locals.

I found my work with the unions satisfying, but Oliver and I had wanted to start a family. I saw myself as a wife and mother, but that didn't mean I wanted to give up my work. For years we had tried to have children, but I had two miscarriages. Then, at last, in 1938, my first child, Karen, was born.

Despite my eagerness, motherhood wasn't easy for me. After the birth I felt depressed. Is motherhood all I want? Oliver, a man liberated long before it became fashionable, encouraged me to work outside the home. He said that I could be both a mother and worker. He knew work was good for my mental health. He said, "Esther, you have a contribution to make. You can make a difference." He made me feel as though I had ability. I think Oliver loved me so much he wanted me to be my own person. He was secure enough in his manliness that he didn't mind having a working wife.

Even with an accepting husband, it isn't easy to combine work and family; it requires a delicate balance and a lot of help from other people. As long as I provided decent labor standards and a fair wage, I didn't have any problem having someone work for me. I never considered the people who worked for me to be servants; they were helpers.

I didn't want to hire someone else to mother my children. I wanted to work, but it was also important to be there for my children. When my children were young, I never took a nine-to-five job; I wanted to be there to see the kids off to school and I wanted to be able to support their activities after school. Those were the terms of my employment; the kids always came first.

I realize how fortunate I have been; I've always had good help. One of our housekeepers, Julia, became a part of the family; she stayed with us for more than 40 years. Except for the period when we were overseas, Julia stayed with us until she died.

I never felt guilty about getting outside help with the children; I didn't mind turning over my wages to someone who helped me out. My only rule was that I tried to earn enough money to pay for the additional help. It didn't always work out that way. One time I was earning $15 a week, and I paid $20 to have someone look after Karen; during that time, Oliver subsidized me.

I began wrestling with these child care issues when I got my first real paying job after Karen was born. It all started when I got a call from Jacob Potofsky, secretary-treasurer of the Amalgamated Clothing Workers. His daughter, Dehlia, had been an intern from Vassar at the summer school; I had met Potofsky when he came to speak at the school. Dehlia introduced us and told her father that I had the kind of "spirit" the union really needed. He looked at me and smiled.

Chapter 4

Disturbing the Peace

In 1938 Jacob Potofsky asked me to join the Amalgamated Clothing Workers. The timing couldn't have been better. Oliver had just taken a job with the Work Projects Administration (WPA) in New York, so we were moving and I needed work. Potofsky introduced me to J. B. S. Hardman, the Amalgamated's director of education, head of the department of cultural activities, and editor of *The Advance*, the union newspaper. Hardman, a very busy man, needed an assistant, and he offered me the job.

This was a very exciting time to be involved with the unions. During this period unions were greatly expanding their reach. Since the National Industrial Recovery Act had passed six years before, workers and unions had been enjoying unprecedented legal support. In particular, Section 7(a) of the act bolstered the strength of the unions by giving employees the right to organize a union for collective bargaining and prohibiting employers from requiring that workers join a company union as a condition of employment. At the Amalgamated, our ranks were strong and our members enthusiastic. Strikes in 1933 by the Amalgamated had brought in 50,000 new members, in addition to forcing higher wages and shorter hours in the clothing industry.

In my new job I taught the garment workers about their rights under their union contracts. After all, people need to know their rights to exercise them. I constantly had to answer the question, "What will the union do for me?" Some workers expressed concern about safety, others worried about speed-ups and toilets and breaks. But the two issues everyone focused on were wages and hours.

My role in the union changed abruptly when, in 1940, President Roosevelt appointed Sidney Hillman, the president of the Amalgamated, to the National Defense Advisory Commission. The war had increased the demand for military clothing, giving more bargaining leverage to the garment workers. Earlier in the war, the US Army had bypassed the unions by giving contracts to the lowest bidders, often tenement sweatshops. But Hillman joined forces with reformer Florence Kelley and together they used their political clout to push for the creation of a Board of Control of Labor Standards. This board was empowered to inspect factories producing army clothing to be sure manufacturers upheld the labor and sanitary standards.

This was an incredible coup. The largest manufacturers of uniforms were the Greif shops, a large men's clothing firm with six plants in Virginia, Pennsylvania, and Delaware. The Greif shops were very anti-union, but they had to unionize or lose their government contracts.

Hillman wanted me to help organize these shops. "Esther, we must have someone who speaks English," he said. Most of the other union organizers were Jews who spoke Yiddish and maybe some broken English. I was one of few who spoke without an accent.

It was an uphill battle the entire way. These workers had been fed anti-union materials for years and years by their employers, but now those same employers welcomed the union and even invited us to hold meetings in the company cafeteria. Suddenly, management needed the unions to continue their government contracts. The power structure had shifted, but the shops had done such a good job of convincing the workers that unions were bad that it was a struggle to get the workers to listen to the advantages of organized labor.

When I first came in, the workers said they would have a union "over their dead bodies." They assumed that all union workers were Bolsheviks, Communists, and Jews. A lot of anti-Semitic and racial slurs were thrown about. We had to walk a very fine line and be careful not to insult the Greif management or the workers. I argued that we were in the middle of a war and that the union was needed to support the war effort. I sold the union by waving the flag—and it helped having the boss on my side.

I appealed to the workers, most of whom were women, by being one of them. I brought my daughter, Karen, who was just a toddler at the time, with me to some of the organizing meetings. I brought her because I didn't want to leave her, and she didn't want me to leave. That was one of the hard parts about being a working mother. But having Karen along turned out to be a very effective organizing tool.

One time we had a meeting in a little church; we always met wherever there was enough room for everyone to sit. I had left Karen with the mother of one of the girls in the shop while I made my speech. Karen felt homesick, so the woman brought her over to the meeting. When Karen appeared in the door, she ran down the aisle, crying, "Mamma! Mamma!"

I hugged her, then she stood by me while I finished my speech. At first I was embarrassed, but these women recognized that I was also a working mother who wanted what's best for my family. My daughter was with me because day care wasn't available. I really understood their needs; I was one of them. We won by an overwhelming margin. In the end, with Karen's help, we organized all six locals.

World War II strengthened the labor movement. Between 1939 and 1941, organized labor signed on nearly 2 million workers. By 1942, the nation was nearly at full employment, building arms and supplies for the US and its allies. The Amalgamated and other unions obtained new members and welcomed new opportunities, but they also needed cautiously to protect high working standards and strong wages.

During the war, we still had to stand tough to negotiate fair contracts. One of my jobs was to keep the crowds under control during contract negotiations. I once said to the crowd, most of whom were women, "When you make bread, you have to put yeast in. Does the bread rise in a minute? No! It takes time. And our negotiators are working on a contract, and that takes time, too."

I used images people could relate to. I compared negotiating a contract to canning vegetables. "When you're working on a contract, you've got to get the lid on tight, just like when you're canning fruits and vegetables. If you don't get the lid down tight, the stuff inside spoils, right? Give the union team the time they need to get the lid on tight."

One method I used was leading the group in song. During one strike, we split the crowd in two groups. One side sang, "You can't get to heaven without a union card," and the other echoed back, "You can try and try, but it's too damn hard."

In addition to the classic labor tunes, we made up our own. The inspiration for another popular song came from the shirtmaker's strike of 1909. Fania Cohn, who was the director of education at the ILGWU, asked me to put a poem she had written to music. I absolutely loved the words. I spoke to Dick Whitmer, who played the piano, and we sat down and put the poem to music. The hardest part was trying to fit in ILGWU. Once we got that, the rest just fell into place. It became one of my favorite union songs:

It was in the black of winter of 1909,
When we froze and bled on the picket line,
We showed the world that women could fight,
And we rose and fought with women's might.
Hail, the waistmakers of 1909
Taking a stand on the picket line,
Breaking the power of those who reign,
Leading the way, breaking the chain.
And we gave new courage to the men,
Who carried on in 1910.
And shoulder-to-shoulder we'll win through,
Led by the ILGWU.

Though the song originated with labor discontent, it was also a genuine women's liberation song.

The unions did a lot to support the war effort. I was involved by serving as vice chair of the Amalgamated Committee on War

Activities, as well as Hillman's representative on Mayor LaGuardia's War Activities Board. For both committees I worked to encourage blood donations. Before the war, most blood banks were open only during the day, making it impossible for many working people to donate blood. We convinced the blood banks to extend their hours to make it easier for working people to participate.

I went into one factory as a union representative in support of the war effort. As soon as the workers saw me, the women reached for their purses to give money, unaware that I was working on a blood drive. I was always struck by the spontaneous generosity of the working people; they were forever willing to share what little they had. Even after a hard day's work, many workers gave blood before heading home.

I recruited blood for both Blacks and Whites. At that time, blood was segregated by race; a lot of people didn't want "Black blood" mixed with White. We had to do a lot of education about how blood is blood, challenging workers to overcome their racism and to support the war effort.

In my discussions, I found that the only way to convince people to accept an integrated blood supply was to get them to use their imagination to take them to the battlefield. I told them, "If your son were on the battlefield and he needed blood to survive, would you take time to ask, 'Is this the blood of a Black man?' Do you want your son to live or die?" Most people would eventually come around, but we didn't convince everyone.

The unions also supported the efforts of the American Red Cross by making their bandage preparation more efficient. The Red Cross volunteers cut and rolled all the bandages by hand, a ridiculous waste of time. I contacted the head of the Clothing Cutters Local Number Four and convinced a crew of volunteers to use their knives and machines to help cut the bandages and increase production. They could cut enough bandages in one night to supply the volunteer bandage rollers for a week.

The racial issue returned during the war because we needed more workers and the only group of workers that had been denied jobs had been the Blacks. For generations, Blacks—especially Black women—had been denied access to good, skilled jobs, but such positions were now open to them. During the war, about 20% of the Black women who had been domestic servants found work in areas where they had previously been snubbed. As White women moved from the laundries into factories, Black women readily took the jobs they left behind.

As part of my job I went with Bessie Hillman, Sidney Hillman's wife, into the shops to help integrate the Black and White workers. Before we could put Black women in a shop, we talked to the women who would sit on both sides of the Black worker to make sure they would accept working next to a Black woman. It was one of the trickiest assignments I had, but again I used patriotism to overcome racism by stressing the need for production to help the war effort.

When I spoke to the women, I asked them why they objected to working with Blacks. "They smell bad."

"Do any of the White girls smell bad?" I asked. They admitted that everyone smells bad sometimes. Their objection was a phony argument based on ignorance. After we talked about it a bit, most women were willing to accept working with Blacks. Of course, a single conversation can't break down a lifetime of racism, but it was a first step toward integration.

It would have been easy for management to make a rule that Blacks would be introduced to the factories and that was that. I can only imagine what kind of resistance and problems that would have created. It doesn't make sense just to make a rule. You have to go in and find out about the workers' concerns, listen to them, and then develop a plan that works for everyone.

There weren't too many Black workers, and the few that existed were men who did most of the hardest, nastiest work, including manning the steam presses. I felt somewhat apprehensive when I tried to convince the workers to accept the Blacks. I couldn't say that it was simply the right thing to do: I had to make an economic argument. "Are you going to let the Blacks undercut your wages?" If they refused to let the Blacks in the union, then the Blacks would get a lower wage and lower the wages for everyone. There was no social or moral message in my words at all. I didn't feel good about that, but I felt I needed just to get the message across.

Even when the Blacks were allowed in the unions, there was a lot of shameful discrimination. We couldn't have a union meeting in the South with Whites and Blacks together. There was quite a bit of controversy surrounding one integrated meeting we did have in Staunton, Virginia. We met in a church, and the Blacks had to sit in the choir seats and the Whites in the pews. We've come a long way since then, but there's still a long way to go.

When I went into the shops to organize, I was appalled by the unsafe working conditions and the lack of training so many women received before they took their jobs. All too often, the women had never been taught how to operate the machinery safely. I heard stories of women who sewed right through their fingers on the big industrial sewing machines. Sometimes the needle would pierce a worker's hand, but she wouldn't know which button to push to make the machine stop. Frantic, she would reach for a knob, but every control she touched would make the machine go faster. In one case, a woman was caught in a sewing machine and had to scream until someone else came and pulled the plug to turn the power off.

In so many cases, it was simply a matter of teaching the workers how to use the equipment, but that took time. In almost every industry, it has taken a tragedy to make employers take the necessary steps to make their equipment safe. It often seems that someone has to die or be severely injured before government forces industry to take preventive safety steps. Now we have the Occupational Safety and Health Administration, but we still need to get employers to protect their workers because it's right, not in response to a tragedy.

I spent a lot of time inside factories. Between the deafening noise, the filthy toilets, and the stuffy rooms, it was easy for union organizers to whip up a lot of antagonism toward the boss. "Look at what he's doing to you! That's not fair!" For a lot of the women it was an empowering process. The women found that together they did have strength. They learned that it sometimes pays to speak up.

For so many women, getting a union meant more than improvements in wages and hours. When working with the shirtworkers in New Haven, Connecticut, we established a union and raised wages to something like 40¢ an hour. After the contract was signed, we had a party. I said to the women, "Isn't it marvelous that we got the wage increase?"

"That's not the most important thing," said one of the women. "The most important reason to have a union is that I won't have to let the boss pat my fanny anymore." Another woman told me she objected to "milkshakes." When I asked what she meant, she told me that her boss would jiggle her breasts and grin and say, "I just want a little milkshake."

I was stunned. It hadn't occurred to me that so many of these women and girls—many were mere teenagers—were sexually exploited on the job. A lot of the foremen wouldn't keep their hands off the women. Before the unions, the women couldn't stand up to their bosses or complain about inappropriate touching. If they objected, they knew they risked having their pay docked for some unfounded charge or they wouldn't get a good work assignment. With the union, the workers could hold their heads high and tell the foreman to go to hell.

The union offered me a lot of support as a woman, and in certain ways I think being a woman helped me as an organizer. It was a profession where it wasn't held against me that I had children. When I was pregnant with Eric in 1939 and with Iver in 1942, Sidney Hillman's wife, Bessie, used to tell me, "Esther, you have the bulge. Don't quit working. It's normal to have the bulge."

Bessie was a fine woman and a powerful labor leader in her own right. She wasn't Sidney Hillman's shadow. She had helped to organize, along with Jane Addams and a lot of wonderful women leaders, the Hart, Schaffner, and Marx strike of 1910. In a speech I once mentioned how wonderful Sidney Hillman was and she told me later, "I was Bessie Abramovitz long before he was Sidney Hillman." They worked together; they were a powerful team.

Bessie was also a practical woman. She once asked me, "Esther, how do you spell cents?"

"Which cents—the money cents or the smell scents?"

"Oh, you intellectuals. What difference does it make?" came her reply.

She taught me a lot about the genuineness of people who have strong feelings, to hell with the trappings. She didn't know how to spell, but she was bright and she was always aware of the world and the big picture. She was one of the most real women I ever met.

She inspired me to do what I wanted and needed to do, regardless of what other people thought. She helped me realize that I didn't need to apologize for having a baby and speaking at a union function—after all, I was both a union organizer and a mother. I spoke at one of the annual conventions and worked my speaking schedule around my nursing schedule. When the union wanted my services, they accommodated my nursing baby.

But being a woman made it harder to work in the union in other ways. In some cases, other union officials seemed to feel they could push me around. There were turf battles. One night I went to Passaic, New Jersey, to address a local. The educational director had sent me in to speak to the union members. After I got back, I was called into the office in New York for a meeting with Tony Froise, the manager of the New Jersey Amalgamated.

He believed he should have absolute control over his membership, and he wanted no one else on his turf. He raked me over the coals, saying I had no right to speak to his union members without his permission.

I told him I was just following orders from the national. He made it clear that *he* was in charge of the New Jersey local and he didn't appreciate me coming into his area one bit. That's when I found out that there were crooked people in the labor movement. Before then, I hadn't been aware that the labor movement had been infiltrated by organized crime. They controlled the truckers and they got a kickback from every shipment. I suppose I had assumed that we were all idealistic socialists. How wrong I was! It's hard to tell how much of his problem was due to my being a woman and how much hinged on the fact that he didn't want anyone—man or woman—spending time on his turf.

Being a woman made my job more difficult when it came to the sexual code among a few of the organizers when they were on the road. One night when I was out of town traveling for the union, I found myself in a very awkward position. After staying up late working, the only space available for the union organizers to sleep was a single room with four or five beds. I took the bed nearest the wall and was disturbed to hear some of the female union members fooling around with a man who was one of the regional representatives from the union. I was an old conservative, not interested in infidelity or extramarital affairs. I felt that a lot of these women had empty lives; they were starved for attention, starved for sex, starved for friendship. I just lay there silently, pretending to be asleep, but I could hear them carrying on. I felt like vomiting, but I didn't know what else to do. I may have been a prude and purist, but I found this behavior unacceptable.

When I got back to New York, I was so haunted by this experience that I wrote an anonymous letter to the union vice president in charge of that area and complained of the behavior. I wrote the letter as though I were a union member and I complained about the bad reputations the union would get if the information got out about the regional union official. I believed in the union, but I thought those people were smut who did the entire movement a disservice. In the end, the union official made a formal apology, but I think that kind of thing continued to go on.

During the 1930s and 1940s, there were a great number of Communists in the labor movement, and I knew a great many of them. These people were no threat to the stability of the United States government; in most cases they were simply idealistic—if impractical—activists.

Many of my peers in the labor movement who were members of the Communist Party tried to recruit me, and I must admit that at times their offers were tempting. They knew how to exploit my feelings that change and reform were happening too slowly in the United States, and even offered me a trip to the Soviet Union to see the party at work.

I felt confused and had many talks with J. B. S. Hardman, director of education at the Amalgamated. I credit him with keeping me from joining the party. He was an old socialist from Russia who fought the Bolsheviks. In Russia his name had been Jacob Slavinsky, which translated into "hard man." He convinced me that communism would not provide the answers I sought. He argued the falsity of the ideology. He said, "Communism is going to collapse. It will be worse than life under the czars. At least you could talk back to the czars."

I wanted change—and I was impatient about wanting it now—but I didn't feel the Communist Party offered answers either. I didn't like the style: We *demand* this and that; I felt uncomfortable with all those demands. It was unrealistic; most of the Communists I knew didn't have their feet on the ground, and they were too hostile for me, too antagonistic.

It wasn't really too long after the Russian Revolution. I read about John Reed and his view of communism as the great hope of the world. I thought some of the ideology was wonderful, but I didn't think it would work in our country. We all discussed these issues at length. In the end, both Oliver and I rejected communism. And, when Roosevelt was elected, we saw the possibility of genuine fulfillment of what we believed in.

The union was always very active in political campaigns, and in 1944 the political action committee of the Committee for Industrial Organization (CIO) sent me to Utah to support Senator Elbert Thomas for re-election. I helped institute "R" Day, Registration Day. We encouraged all union members and their families to register to vote. We also set up some of the first telephone banks. I got the telephone company to give us 10 lines, and we set up the phones in Carpenters' Hall in Salt Lake City. We got women auxiliary members to come in and call every union member. We started in the heavily Democratic areas, then moved out from there. We also had a sound truck. We'd have runners go around for several blocks, getting crowds to gather, and then we'd have speakers come.

"Do you want your children to have a decent education? Do you want to have a job?" We pulled the crowds together, then gave them all the good reasons they should vote for Senator Thomas and President Roosevelt. We all believed in the New Deal, and we won.

Because of my connections in Utah, I got a call from David Dubinsky of the ILGWU. It was during the summer, and I wasn't working full time for the Amalgamated.

He said, "We need a Mormon organizer in Utah." Some factories in Los Angeles had been organized, so the shopowners picked up and moved to Salt Lake City, where there was no union. I called my mother and my sister and I asked if they would help me take care of the kids if I accepted the job. My mother was delighted to have me at home, so I took the kids to Utah for two months, leaving Oliver in New York working for the WPA.

When I arrived in Utah, I was struck by how little I knew about the working conditions in my home state before I returned as a union organizer. If I had known what had been going on in my home state earlier, I would have risen up earlier. To a large degree, I was isolated when I lived in Utah, even though my family lived only a few miles from the working-class families. It wasn't until years later that I learned that so much of the anti-union sentiment came from the fact that the Mormon Church owned many of the mines and factories that exploited the workers. And the church didn't want any competing authority—loyalty must be to the church, not to the union.

When I came home an activist, my eyes were opened. First, I went to KSL, the largest radio station in Salt Lake City, and asked to buy time.

"What for?" asked the salesman.

I told him I was an organizer for the garment workers and that I wanted to explain to people the need for a union.

"We don't need any help from outsiders," came his reply.

"I'm not an outsider. I was born and raised in Utah."

"Who are you?"

"Esther Eggertsen."

"You're not Lars Eggertsen's daughter, are you?" Without waiting for a reply, he continued, "You should be ashamed of yourself. You're nothing better than a disturber of the peace."

The radio station wouldn't sell me any time. I went from door to door working up support. With every call, I had to explain that I was raised a Mormon, not an outsider. I know being from Utah really helped. We established a union later that summer, with a great deal of help from the newly established National Labor Relations Board.

When I got back to New York I found that Hillman was very angry with me for having helped out the ILGWU. "If you want to organize, organize for the Amalgamated," he said.

"But Sidney," I reminded him, "you always taught me that the most important thing is to organize." He was mad for a time; then all was forgiven.

I made another trip to Utah later that year on behalf of the CIO political action committee. At the time, John L. Lewis, president of the miners' union, was urging people to vote for Dewey, not FDR. I was working for the clothing workers and we were part of the CIO group. As I was from Utah, they sent me back to make the case for Roosevelt.

I went to Eureka, a mining town. I could find the town on a map, but I don't think I had ever met anyone who lived there. I went to a meeting with the miners and they said, "What are you, a woman, doing here?"

"Look, she's a Mormon and she's from Utah," came the reply from Jack Kroll, who was the head of the CIO political action committee. I didn't mind claiming my Mormon roots at times like this. I didn't consider it hypocritical; after all, this was my community, and Utah was my first home.

After he came to my defense, they listened to me, and we argued over FDR. During one discussion someone said, "John L. Lewis can take care of our wages and working conditions, but he isn't the best one to tell us who to choose for president of the United States." In the end, the union supported Roosevelt. I was very proud of that.

That night, I was invited to a party given by the women's auxiliary for the miners. Early on, I made a speech about the importance of the women's support for Roosevelt. Then things got lively. Here I was a good Mormon girl on my own turf, but I was shocked: At one point during the party, a group of four or five women put on men's long underwear and had carrots hanging out of the flies. They danced around the room, wiggling their carrots and laughing. I didn't know quite how to react, so I just laughed along with the rest of them. I couldn't say anything without isolating myself. If I hadn't gone along with the joke, I would have undone everything I had done that day in winning the support of their husbands. That incident helped teach me an important lesson: You have to keep your mouth shut and keep your mind on the final goal.

In 1944 our family moved to Washington, DC, and I became a lobbyist for the Amalgamated. When I first reported for my job, I walked into a meeting at the old CIO headquarters at Jefferson Square. The meeting included lobbyists from all the major industries, including the auto workers, the rubber workers, and the steel workers. The men sat around a table; when I entered the room, they stood up. I knew I didn't want to be treated differently. I said, "Please don't stand up for me. I don't intend to stand up for you."

A lot of the men weren't comfortable having a woman working with them on Capitol Hill. Phil Murray, the wonderful president of the CIO, later told me that after that meeting a group of the lobbyists went to him and asked, "What are we going to do with Esther?" The practice at the time was to assign a lobbyist to a legislator to keep him informed on union issues and, in a way, to keep tabs on him. Someone said, "Give her to Kennedy; he won't amount to much." It was one of the best breaks I ever had.

At that time, John F. Kennedy was a brand-new representative from Boston and not very well liked by labor because he had not offered adequate support to certain civil rights bills. He served on the Labor Committee and over the years I saw him grow.

When I first accepted the assignment to cover Kennedy, I went to his office to get acquainted. I liked him immediately; he asked good questions. From the time of our first meeting I felt that he was a secure human being. He could ask simple questions without being afraid of showing what he didn't know. He was restless with weak answers, and he could dodge and duck tough issues with the best (or worst) in Congress.

A lot of people in the labor movement thought Kennedy was born with a silver spoon in his mouth and that he couldn't understand working people. But he did understand. I realized that when I helped him get ready for a hearing on an amendment to the Fair Labor Standards Act to raise the minimum wage. I could tell by the kinds of questions he asked that he knew the issues. He probably understood the issues a lot better than many people with working-class backgrounds.

Kennedy once quizzed me about the Norris-LaGuardia Act, a law that deprived the federal courts of the power to prohibit certain types of union activity and collective acts that could be performed by the individual. He wouldn't let up until he thoroughly understood the issue.

When I was working on Capitol Hill, one of my main projects was attempting to raise the minimum wage from 40¢ to 75¢ an hour. When the minimum wage first took effect in 1939, it was 25¢. It was important for the unions to raise the minimum wage so they could raise their contract wage. The unions always got just a little bit more than the minimum wage. They needed the law to provide the floor, and they'd inch up a little bit higher.

During the hearings on the minimum wage, we heard from someone at a large restaurant chain about why they felt they should be allowed to pay potato peelers and the kitchen help less than minimum wage. During the discussion, one of the senators asked the question, "What is worth? How do you measure worth?" In response, the restaurant spokesman said that potato peelers were worth less than minimum wage. The senator said, "But if you don't have potato peelers, you can't run a restaurant." Eventually the man from the restaurant chain had to admit that the potato peelers were paid less than minimum wage because they were willing to accept less: "I pay less because I can get them for less." He made the point better than I ever could have.

The first year I was working on the issue, we got the bill through both sides of Congress; then it was wrecked by an amendment added at the last minute that killed the minimum wage. I called Hillman in tears. He said, "Esther, congratulations. We got it to the floor this time. Next time we'll get it through." We did. It was a very important lesson.

Over time, I picked up a lot of the subtleties of lobbying. I spoke to House Speaker Sam Rayburn about how I had tried to pin someone down about a decision he had made. He said, "Esther, never say that. Remember this: 'It's not me; it's not thee, it's the man behind the tree.'" He was right: When negotiating or trying to convince someone of your point of view, always leave the other person a way to save face.

We were also having a lot of trouble at that time with workers who were not covered by the Fair Labor Standards Act. For example, there were Blacks who harvested brush from the woods to make plywood and other wood products; they were paid by the load, getting less than the minimum wage because their employers called them "independent contractors" and "entrepreneurs." All kinds of silly terms were used to get around the law.

I made a number of speeches about the extension of coverage under the Fair Labor Standards Act, and I started using a catchy gimmick. I would hold up a piece of paper that I said represented workers who should be covered by the act. I would then name a group that was excluded, such as the retail workers, and I would tear off a piece of the paper. After going through the entire list of groups exempted from coverage, the paper was little more than a pile of scraps. It was very effective; people understood my point.

I also used a true story I learned during a discussion of the extension of coverage to the retail workers: A salesclerk in an exclusive women's shop described her long hours and low pay and asked why she was not covered by the act. When it was explained to her that she didn't work in interstate commerce, the girl quickly responded, "Look, I sell Mrs. Roosevelt her underwear, and you can't tell me that what she wears isn't in interstate commerce."

We all had a good laugh, but progress on extending coverage was moving far too slowly. At the same time, I was working to get the wage-rate raised. I was pregnant with my fourth child, and as the debate dragged on, I got bigger and bigger. One of the biggest arguments against the bill was that it was inflationary. Senator Wayne Morse of Oregon joked, "Esther, don't tell me that bill won't be inflationary—just look at you!"

Senator Claude Pepper of Florida chimed in, "If the baby is a boy, call him 'Maxie' for maximum hours, and if it's a girl, call her 'Mini' for minimum wage." Despite the senator's admonition during the campaign, we didn't name my son Maxie—we named him Lars.

Peterson in 1934 while teaching at the Bryn Mawr Summer School.

Peterson, at far right, was recruited by the International Ladies Garment Workers Union in 1941 to organize a clothing company plant in Salt Lake City. Here union organizers and representatives of the clothing company celebrate the contract signing.

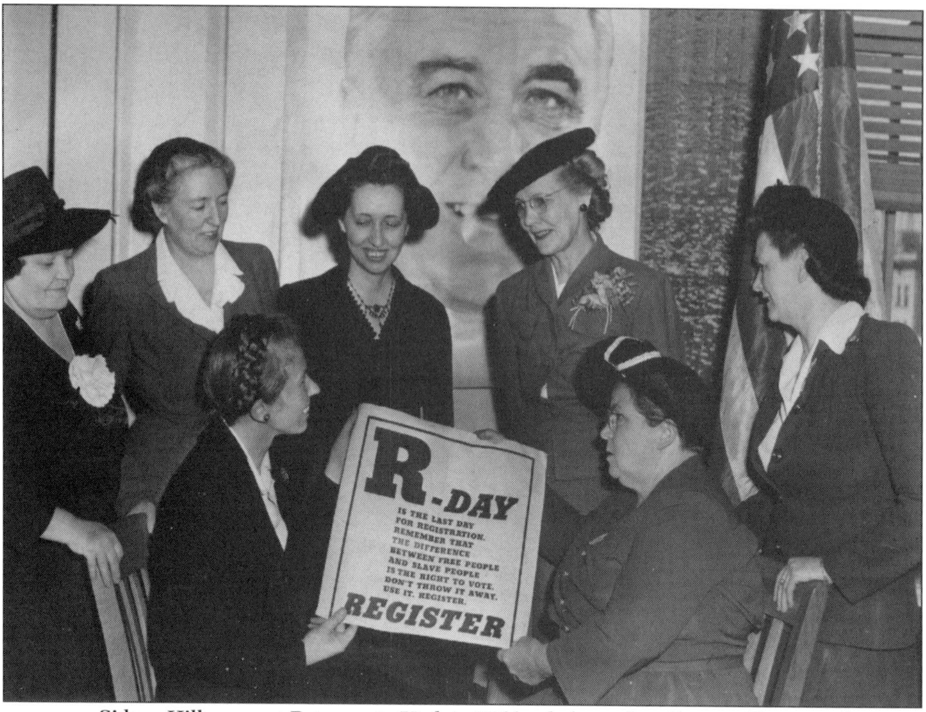

SCHLESINGER LIBRARY, RADCLIFFE COLLEGE

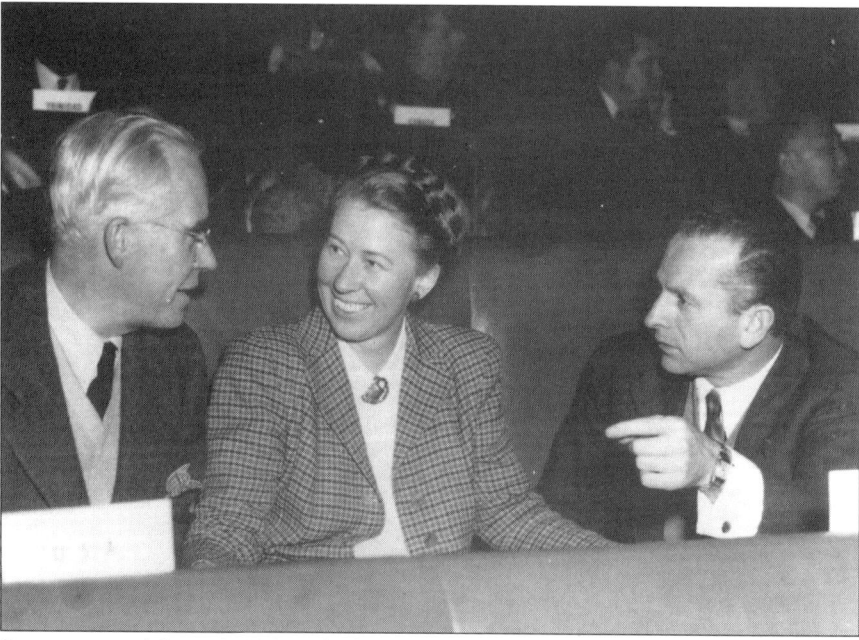

Sidney Hillman sent Peterson to Utah in 1944 to help re-elect Senator Thomas, who supported organized labor. She initiated R Day to encourage women to register to vote.

Peterson was a delegate in 1949 to the first meeting of the International Confederation of Free Trade Unions, held in London.

In 1953 Peterson helped set up the first international school for working women, modeled after the Bryn Mawr summer school. From left: Mrs. Edwards, London; Mrs. Isakson, Sweden; Mrs. Nungat, India; Esther Peterson, Stockholm; Mrs. Williamson, Stockholm.

The International School for Women in Belgium, August 1956. Peterson is in the back row, fifth from the left.

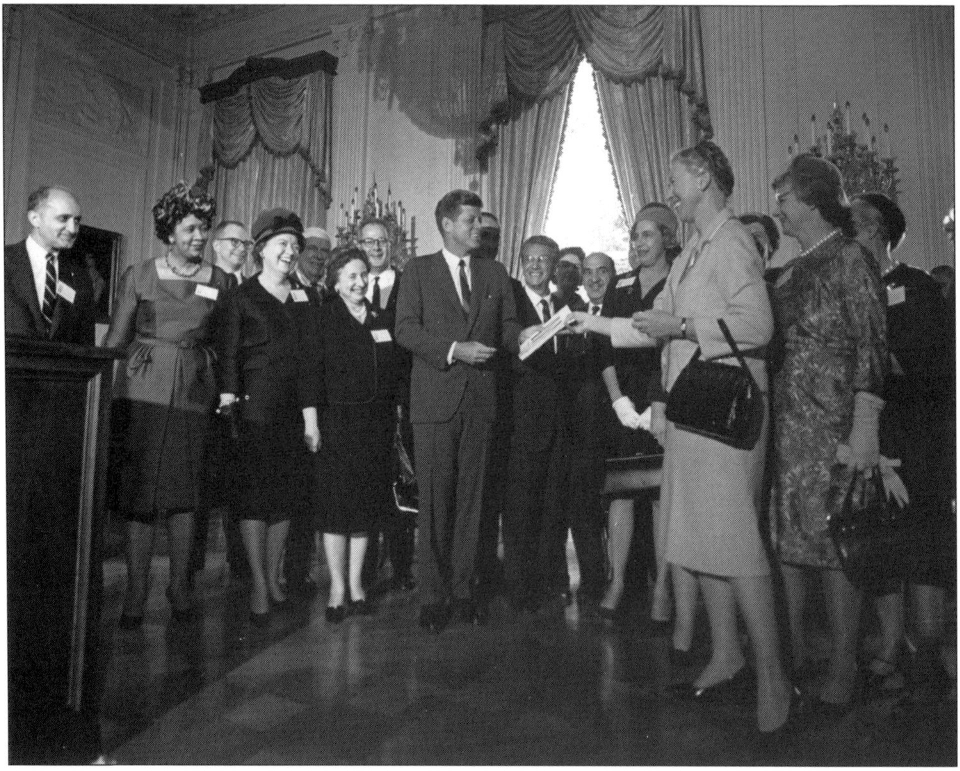

PHOTO BY ASSOCIATED PRESS

Peterson, Secretary of Labor Arthur Goldberg, and members of the President's Commission on the Status of Women report to President Kennedy on the establishment of the commission on December 14, 1961.

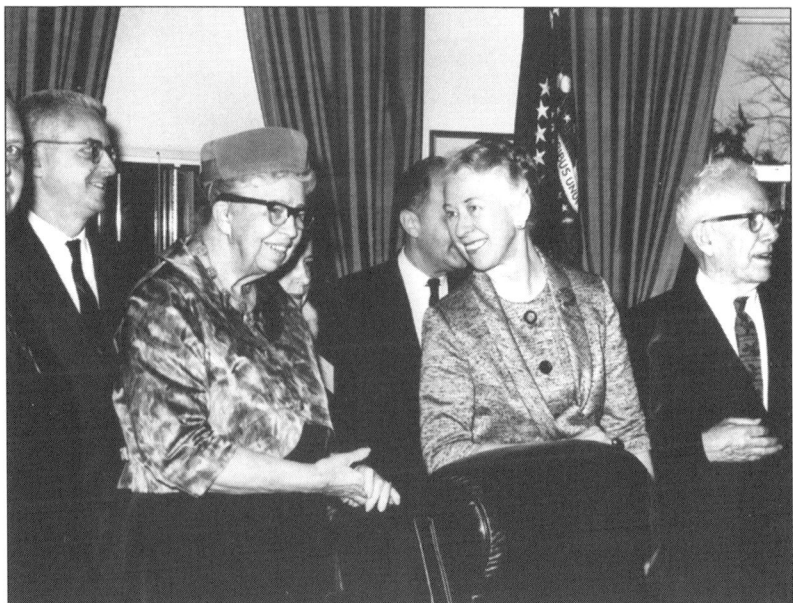

Peterson with Eleanor Roosevelt (left) when they were working together on the President's Commission on the Status of Women.

Peterson with her good friend Dorothy Height, head of the National Council of Negro Women, in 1963.

Left, Peterson presents the Equal Pay Bill to Vice-President Johnson in February 1963 on Capitol Hill. Johnson made it an administration bill.

Below, Peterson in her office with Dick Cohen at the Labor Department when she was director of the Women's Bureau under President Kennedy. Portraits of Peterson's heroines decorate the walls.

President Johnson and Peterson in 1963, driving to his ranch in Texas, where he appointed her special assistant to the president for consumer affairs.

Peterson checks produce quality as special assistant to the president for consumer affairs in 1965.

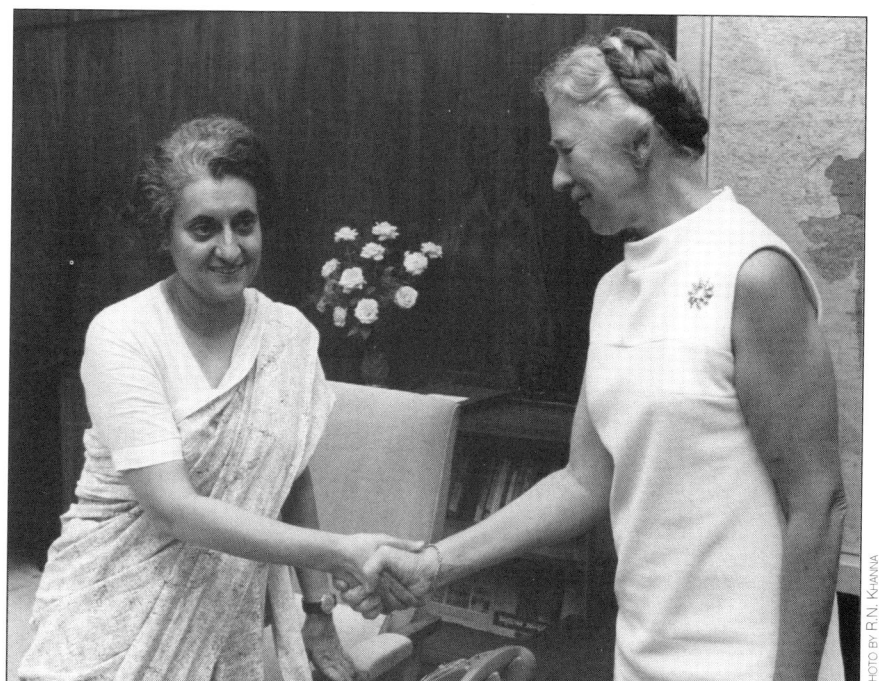

Peterson meets Indira Ghandi in 1969. She was asked by the US government to travel to India on behalf of the US Information Service to represent labor, the women's movement, and consumer affairs.

Peterson as consumer adviser to Giant Food, Inc. With her is Paul Forbes, special assistant to the president of Giant.

Peterson receives honorary degree from Northwestern University. She has received a total of 13 honorary degrees.

Peterson (sitting next to President Carter) and other consumer rights leaders meet with Carter to lobby for a consumer bill.

On nomination night in 1980, Peterson celebrates President Carter's re-election nomination with (from left to right) Bill Strauss, President Carter, Peterson, and Mayor of Los Angeles Bradley.

Peterson receives the Presidential Medal of Freedom from President Carter on January 16, 1981.

Peterson receives a Lifetime Achievement Award from the Foundation for Hospice and Homecare in 1990. From left: Bill Halamandaris, The Hon. Frank Moss, Peterson, and Val Halamandaris.

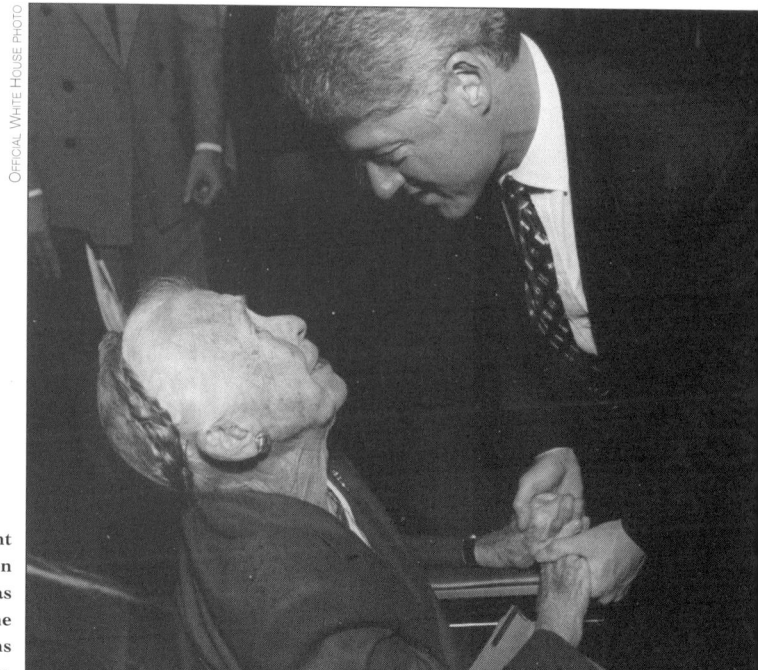

In 1993 President Bill Clinton named Peterson as a delegate to the United Nations General Assembly.

Peterson's efforts in the consumer movement brought her and the movement public visibility, as evidenced by these cartoons that have been dedicated to Peterson by the artists, George Basset, *left*, and Charles Schulz, *above*.

Esther (right) and neighbor Jenny Mae Edler, ca. 1918.

The Eggertsen family, ca. 1925. Seated left to right: Anna Marie, Esther's mother, Mark, Esther's father, and Esther; standing left to right: Thelma, Luther, and Algie.

Peterson sharing her love of music with her chidren, ca. 1950.

The Peterson family in 1954 when they were living in Brussels. Clockwise from the bottom: Oliver, the family pet Vicky, Lars, Eric, Karen, Iver, and Esther. This photo became the family's Christmas card that year.

Esther and Oliver Peterson in the study of their home in Arlington, Virginia. Peterson was assistant secretary of labor and director of the Women's Bureau at the time.

The Peterson family in December 1961 in Arlington, Virginia. From left: Eric, Iver, Lars, Esther, Vicky the dog, Oliver, and Karen.

Peterson and her grandchildren, ca. 1980.

Peterson and Oliver take their grandsons Joshua (Karen's son) and Oliver (Eric's son) for a walk at their farm in Vermont in 1972.

Oliver and Esther Peterson in 1973.

Chapter 5

Uprooted

We really weren't the foreign service types, but when Oliver was contacted by the State Department about becoming a diplomat, we certainly were interested in knowing more about it. At the time, the State Department was trying to beef up its expertise in labor. Before then, the foreign service had primarily consisted of the well-educated and the privileged, who had no contact with labor. But in the late 1940s the Truman administration realized the importance of the Cold War struggle between the emerging free trade unions and those manipulated by Communists. Labor governments were emerging, and as Oliver had a lot of experience with the labor movement, he was an attractive candidate and was welcomed as one of the first labor attachés.

Before the State Department could offer us a post, Oliver had to undergo an extensive FBI investigation. The FBI officers questioned our friends, neighbors, and family. They went to Washington State and interviewed Oliver's mother and stepfather, asking countless questions about their support for Harry Bridges. They even questioned folks who lived near us at the farm in Vermont, where a neighbor said, "Anyone who can swing an ax like Oliver can't be bad." The only word against us was from neighbors in Vermont who objected to the fact that we had loaned the farm to some friends who had gone to a local brook and gone skinny-dipping. In this case, skinny-dipping didn't prove to be a federal offense. Oliver passed these hurdles and was approved, but our left-wing friends would come back to haunt us later.

At first the State Department offered us a post in India. We read the post report and decided it was too dangerous a place to take four small children; there was so much disease and the water had to be boiled. We couldn't even eat the fresh vegetables; it seemed as though there were just too many dangers. Oliver was then offered a post as labor attaché in Sweden, which we gladly accepted.

We were both delighted to have the opportunity to spend time close to our homelands. We understood more about the culture and traditions there. Oliver could speak and understand Norwegian because his parents spoke it at home. He didn't even speak English until he was six years old and started school. When he learned Swedish, he was told he spoke it with a Norwegian accent.

In preparation for service abroad, I underwent the hat-and-gloves protocol training from the State Department. I learned the proper way to turn down an invitation, to use a fish fork, to wear a hat and veil. I felt frustrated that the focus of the training was on the intricacies of etiquette, not a bit of practical information on what I was in for. My training session had nothing to do with everyday living—not a word about what to wear, how to say hello, how to understand the culture of the place where I was going to live for four years. Before leaving the US, we bought the kids a lot of heavy winter clothes, but when we got there the kids wanted to wear Swedish clothes. They didn't want to stand out. They wanted to wear the sweaters and the knit caps with the tassels on the ends like the ones the other kids wore. The State Department never told us about the social traditions and the practical skills for living.

I wasn't a white-gloves person, but I did make my bow to protocol. I was told when I had to wear a hat, and I said, "But I never wear a hat." The wise woman advising me then replied, "Just be yourself." I compromised: I got a little hairband with an attached veil that would fit in front of my braids. I actually had a red one and a black one. It wasn't really a hat, but it served the purpose.

We left Washington in November, so we had to arrange to take the children out of school. Their teachers were so supportive and understanding about helping the kids through the transition, not just to another school but to another country. As it could be more than a month before the kids got into their new schools, the teachers designed lesson plans and I taught the kids so they wouldn't get behind. Before leaving I threw a party for the kids' teachers. Once the teachers arrived, I offered them tea and coffee.

My son Iver's teacher responded, "Where's the beer and whiskey?"

I didn't know what to say, so I stammered, "If you want some I'll get it."

"Oh, I prefer coffee," she said, before explaining that the other day in class during a discussion on nutrition, she asked each member of the class what he or she drank at home.

Iver answered, "Beer and whiskey." When she asked him why he had said that, he answered, "Oh, everyone said 'milk' and I wanted to be different." Iver—my dear little Iver, all of six years old—was always an original.

We started our trip on November 5, 1948, the day after the presidential election. We had stayed up late packing the night before, listening on the radio to the poll results showing that Truman was winning. I had been so sure that Truman was going to win that I had placed a $10 bet on him—my first real bet. Before the election I had been campaigning, and I felt the momentum growing behind him. What a send-off victory!

It was an exciting night, and early the next morning we left for Sweden via New York on the Swedish boat, the *Gripsholm*. During the 10-day trip we were all seasick except Iver, who went down to have breakfast at the captain's table every morning while the rest of us stayed in our cabin. We joked that Iver had Viking blood in his veins.

The kids had a marvelous time on board. One night Karen won at Bingo; we organized games on the deck to keep the children occupied. On board this Swedish ship, the language and music were different. The children immediately noticed the difference and commented, "Golly, you should hear the little kids. They can all talk Swedish fast as anything. Gee, they're smart."

At that time it seemed that the plumbing was the most exciting thing in those kids' lives. The kids had never seen a bidet. When I went into the bathroom, Karen was ready to give Lars, the baby, a bath in the bidet. When I stopped her she asked, "What's a bidet? Is that a thing to wash a baby in?" Another responded without hesitation, "No, it's a thing to wash the baby *out!*"

We didn't expect any kind of welcome when we arrived in Sweden. We didn't know any of the people from the embassy, although we did know a few Swedish women workers who had attended the Bryn Mawr Summer School on scholarship from the American-Scandinavian Society. For years I had corresponded with one former student, Greta Hudin. I told her that we were going to be spending time in Sweden and let her know when we were arriving. We landed in Gothenburg, then drove up to Stockholm. When we were crossing a bridge through town there stood Greta, waving and welcoming us to her country. She had waited for hours for us to pass.

Greta proved to be an invaluable friend; she helped us get through a lot of difficult transitions. We stayed at Saltsjobaden, a fancy hotel, while our house in Nockeby was being prepared. A fancy hotel is no place to stay with four small children. We had to dress for dinner each night—Oliver wore a tuxedo and I wore a long dress. The dinner tables were set with six knives and six forks. Understanding the high-brow rules of etiquette was too much to ask of kids; we were satisfied if they would use a single set of silverware correctly. Several times during dinner, Lars, the baby, would have to go to the bathroom, so Oliver would have to traipse back and forth through the dining room escorting him.

My fondest memories of the hotel involved the big bay window in our suite. The window had a curtain in front, and the kids would put on plays, using the window as a stage. But the stage wasn't enough to keep us content. We kept up with the routine for about a week, then decided it didn't make any sense to stay there with the children.

We decided to move into the house before our furniture arrived. Greta and some other students helped us collect cots and bedding and dishes from the "Tempo," the Swedish five-and-10, and we camped in our house. We had a rug on the living room floor and a table in the entrance, and we got by.

One night I asked all the girls whom I had taught at the summer school over for dinner and I used our treasured Swedish silverplate, which Oliver had given me when Iver was born. It was a simple, plain pattern, but very beautiful. One of the girls offered to get me more; she was now working as an inspector at the silver factory that made it, so she was able to get me a lot of good seconds at discount prices. I soon had enough silverware for the fancy diplomatic parties, and I couldn't tell the difference between the firsts and seconds.

As part of the foreign service protocol, we were to make a diplomatic call to the home of the ambassador. We were to call on all the people above us in the diplomatic hierarchy and leave a card engraved, "Oliver A. Peterson, Labor Attaché." If you turned down the corner before leaving the card that meant it had been delivered personally. If the person you were visiting wanted to meet you, you were invited in. If they didn't care to meet you, you simply left your card to let them know you had paid your respects.

We had dressed the kids in their finest clothes before making our rounds so that we would make a good impression. But our hearts sank when we were greeted by Ambassador Freeman Matthews, his wife—and his huge doberman pincher. The dog jumped up on Karen, who instinctively swatted the dog and said in a stern voice, "You don't do that."

Oliver and I both thought that was the end, but the dog walked over and sat down by Karen and she began to pet it and talk to it. The ambassador was impressed; he introduced the dog, Big Ben, to Karen and invited her to come over and train him. The dog later sired some puppies, and the ambassador gave Karen the pick of the litter. She named her dog Prince, and what a dog he was. He used to follow Karen to school and wait for her until the day was over.

We were still settling into our new home when the holidays approached. The kids had been worried: Will Santa find us? He's a different man over here. Instead of losing out on our old traditions, we developed new ones. On December 13, Oliver and I had been out to a party and Greta had stayed with the children. Very early the next morning, when Oliver and I were sound asleep on our borrowed army cots, the door opened and in came a great apparition of light. I looked up and saw my beautiful 10-year-old Karen entering the room with a wreath of candles in her golden red hair. Our three sons followed behind her carrying candles. They were singing a Swedish song in celebration of Lucia.

I thought I had died and was entering heaven, greeted by my children as angels. I then learned that this was part of a Swedish celebration of light that takes place on the longest night of the year. According to tradition, in the 13th century Swedish sailors were shipwrecked off the coast of Italy, and in the middle of the night the angel Saint Lucia appeared to them and guided them to safety. Greta had set the whole thing up while we had been out. The celebration has since become a family tradition, only now it is one of my grandchildren who serves as Lucia, the Promise of Light and Good Things to Come. It marks the beginning of the Christmas season, a season of promise and hope.

While stationed in Sweden, we often took short family trips, sometimes to learn more about our family's history. We visited Denmark and learned that during World War II our families used a weather vane to point to where the Germans were staying that night. We also found that the Danes wore safety pins on their lapels to symbolize solidarity; they were sticking together.

When we took a trip to Norway to visit Oliver's roots, we stopped at the home of a distant relative who had a beautiful handwoven rug on the floor. The design was very interesting, with flecks of red scattered throughout. I asked about the rug and Oliver's distant aunt said, "The red comes from the insignias we picked off the German soldiers' uniforms when they retreated. We wove them into the rugs so that we could walk on them for the rest of our lives."

In Sweden we did our best to fit in with the community; we didn't want to isolate ourselves by associating only with other diplomatic families within the embassy compound. We shopped at the Konsum, the local co-op, although this practice raised eyebrows among other diplomatic wives. Some people criticized us for using the co-op by saying, "You just don't shop at the co-op; that's a socialist place. It's for the working people." We would proudly respond, "We are the working people." We lived in the ritzy section of Stockholm, but our universe was much wider. We were really much more like the social democratic Swedes than the conservative diplomats. Some embassy people thought we were a little odd, but we were in Sweden to get to know the workers. This was the life we were used to.

I had a lot of fun overcoming the cultural barriers. I remember going to the butcher and trying to ask for a rump roast. I didn't know how to say "rump roast," so I let out a big "Moooo," then hit my rump. The butcher understood, and I got just what I wanted.

There were differences in how Americans and Swedes shopped. Most of the Swedes would shop at different stores for different products, which meant separate trips to the butcher, the baker, and the dairy. I didn't have time to go marketing every day, so I brought along a big basket to stock up on the things we needed. In the checkout line I heard a little girl ask, *"Har det dvinnor hotellet?"* Does that woman run a hotel?

The co-op issue was nothing compared to the scandal involving our rent. When I found out the horrendously high rent the embassy was paying for us to rent our house, I spoke to the neighbors and they said we were paying much too much. I wrote to the man who rented the house to us, and he had a lawyer come out to see us. He said, "What are you so concerned about? You aren't paying for it."

"Yes, I am," I responded. "I'm an American taxpayer."

Oliver and I took the case to a hearing before a local rent-control official, and we won. My Swedish friends loved it, but some of the affluent class never forgave us.

We learned a lot about Sweden from friends we entertained at parties. One of the first parties we gave was a spaghetti dinner for the workers at the food co-op. We were told that the party couldn't be considered an official function. If it were an official party, we could submit a bill and be reimbursed, but this was basically a social party; we were getting to know the local people and brushing up on our Swedish. It bothered me that we could have a party for the top labor officials and their wives, but we couldn't formally entertain store employees. It was a reciprocal social exchange: We taught them the Virginia Reel and they taught us the Hambo.

One night I also learned a lot about Swedish etiquette. Our kitchen faced the front of our house, and as I was getting ready for dinner I could see people arriving. Guests were invited for 7:00, which in my book means people arrive sometime after 7:00. Not in Sweden. At the kitchen window, 10 minutes before 7:00, I saw people walking up and down the street with flowers, waiting to come in. I ran upstairs to change clothes so that I could breathlessly answer the door. After a few dinners, we started inviting people "anytime between 7:00 and 7:30," so our guests would be more relaxed and avoid the mad rush at the appointed hour.

The kids stared down from the top of the stairs at the guests as they arrived. At one party it had been quite cold; the women took off their coats, then pulled off their snuggies or long underwear. The children giggled, "Mamma, the women are taking off their pants!" Our guests slipped off their snuggies and stuffed them into the sleeves of their coats with their mittens.

I enjoyed entertaining, both the high-ranking embassy big shots and the Swedish workers. I had a hard time with some of the foreign service women who didn't treat working people very well. I once went to tea at one of the women's houses and there was something on the floor. The hostess, who was actually the spouse of one of the lower level officers, rang a bell and had a servant come in. She said, "That's smutsig. It shouldn't be here." I had to bite my tongue to stop from saying, "If it's dirty, pick it up yourself and throw it in the wastebasket."

So many of the women were concerned with social connections—who had tea with whom. I got real pleasure from the day I took the tram into town. I wasn't sure where to get off, so I asked the woman sitting next to me, who happened to speak some English. We got to talking and it turned out she was a schoolteacher who taught mathematics. I later found out that she was Aina Erlander, the prime minister's wife. We became good friends, and when we would attend social functions I could feel the envy from the other wives when I would be greeted by name. I felt good because we got to know the Swedish hierarchy through the Swedish people, not through the embassy.

My other complaint about the embassy officials was their lack of concern for family matters. I'll never forget the night we almost lost Iver. He and a friend had been ice skating on a nearby lake, and Iver had fallen through a hole that had been created by an ice fisherman. His friend had pulled him out and dragged him home on a sled. He had a big, heavy sheepskin coat on, which probably saved his life. We waited until we knew he was himself, then left for the party.

At the party, one of the diplomats asked us why we were so late. After we explained the situation he turned to me and said, "Isn't it more important that you tend to your husband's career? The boy was all right; he got out."

I was shocked at his attitude. I didn't want to go to the party at all. That man didn't realize that I was making a real sacrifice by going to the party late. I felt that I belonged at home with Iver.

We wanted to put the kids in *Alston Folkskola*, the Swedish public schools, but we ran into a lot of difficulty. Most of the diplomats' children attended a private international French school inside the "golden ghetto." We wanted the kids to get a genuine Swedish education, but the teachers were very harsh. Several teachers publicly humiliated the children, thinking that this would make them learn Swedish faster. It was hard enough to send the kids to school—it was dark in the mornings when they left for school and dark in the afternoon when they arrived home—but I wouldn't stand for them to be treated poorly in class.

It was a big mistake. The kids didn't speak Swedish, so we hired a tutor to teach them after school. One day one of the kids came home from school and told me he wet his pants in class. He said that he had tried to tell the teacher he had to go to the bathroom, but she wouldn't listen because he couldn't say so in Swedish. Another teacher yelled at Karen in front of her classmates. When I spoke to the teacher after school about the matter, he told me that he thought Karen would learn faster if he was harsh with her in class.

In a third episode, Eric came home with a red mark on his face. I asked him what happened and he said that the teacher hit him. He had several friends with him, and they said, "It's not his fault." It seems the teacher thought someone was pushing in line, and assumed it had been Eric. In a rage, I went to the school and confronted the teacher. I told him that Eric said he didn't do it, and even if Eric did do something wrong, teachers have no business slapping children. When I got home, Eric's friends were stunned that I would defend my child to the teacher. They told Eric, "I can't believe your mother did that. My mother would say, 'The teacher is right,' even if I didn't do it." I've always believed my children, and they've always earned and deserved my trust.

After things didn't work out with the public schools, the kids transferred to Swedish private schools. We had wanted to avoid the elitism of the private schools, but we weren't willing to prove a point at our children's expense. In the end, the kids all learned to speak Swedish fluently. When we returned to the United States, they sometimes enjoyed walking down the street speaking Swedish, so people would assume they didn't understand English.

My experiences with Swedish public schools were not all bad. In Sweden they had lovely nursery schools every block or so. When it was time to put my youngest, Lars, in nursery school, I went to a nearby school and met with the teacher, who spoke a little English. I was worried about sending Lars somewhere where he couldn't communicate with the other children, but the teacher assured me that she could work it out.

I came back the next morning, and the kids were sitting in a circle. The teacher said in Swedish, "This is Lars, the boy I told you about." She showed the children where Lars came from on a map and then she said, "He will be saying the same things you say, but it will sound different. But there are words that sound the same, like 'come.' We say 'koom.'"

Right then a little girl reached out her hand and said, "Koom, Lars." He joined the other children in the circle, and I was overwhelmed by the acceptance of these little children. It was one of my most touching memories of Sweden. I went home and cried.

The kids had no trouble making friends. Karen came home the first day of school carrying a flower given to her by a new friend. The next day the neighbor girl who had given her the flower walked with Karen to school. In fact, the other kids loved coming to our house, the American house. We had snacks and were quite casual. Many Swedish homes were much more formal.

One of our neighbors had a son, Christian, who often played with the boys. His father once told me, "If nothing else, Christian should get a good mark in his English studies." But when the grades were posted, he failed English! His teacher told him, "You're speaking American, not English."

Socializing is part of the job when serving as a diplomatic family. Not long after we arrived in Sweden, I was invited to an early dinner party. I wanted to get the kids fed and ready for bed before leaving, so I asked the hostess if I could come a little late. She told me that she had settled on an early hour so that she could avoid paying overtime to the domestic workers she had hired to help with the party. I had never heard of such a thing. I then learned about the Swedish domestic labor law, which established standards, restrictions on hours, and overtime provisions for domestic workers.

I was fascinated with the concept and wanted to do a study on the need for standards for domestic workers in the US. When we were on leave and visiting the US, I spoke to some people at the Women's Bureau of the US Department of Labor, and they asked me to do a study of the Swedish system. By contrast, in the US our domestic workers weren't even covered by the Fair Labor Standards Act. Domestic workers—along with the laundry workers, the agricultural workers, and the retail workers—have always been among the left-out people who are the last to be protected by federal labor laws.

I collected both hard data and anecdotes about domestic work in Sweden. The final report, "Toward Domestic Employment," was published in 1950, but before publication, an editor turned it into governmentese and threw out most of my anecdotes and cartoons. It was particularly appropriate for me to write about *hemvardarinna*, the "mother substitutes" or "homewatchers." While I was working on the report, I slipped and hurt my knee. I couldn't get out of bed, so I called the social agency and asked for help from a mother substitute.

The woman came and took over my responsibilities. I began to investigate the practice. I went to witness the training and learned what their duties were. In the north, they were given a "wilderness bonus" because they might have to milk cows and do more work under tougher conditions. In one moving case, a mother had died and left four small children. When the mother substitute arrived, she asked, "Did your mother have an apron?" The children showed her where it was. She put it on and asked the children, "What did your mother do with you to have a good time?" They told her that they made candy, so they made caramels together.

Of course, there is no real substitute for a mother, but these women did more than keep the kids clean and out of trouble; they did their best to mother them. It was a great way for middle-aged women who didn't work full time to make a little extra money and to feel useful. It was a way of assigning value to women's traditional skills. It was an inspiring use of the talents and resources of older women. It was so refreshing to see the recognition of the social and economic value of "women's work." This approach stood in stark contrast with our attitudes in the US. This difference kept coming back to me in the form of an old nursery rhyme we used to sing while jumping rope when I was a child:

I wish I had a nickel, I wish I had a dime,
I wish I had a sweetheart to love me all the time.
I'd have her wash the dishes, I'd have her scrub the floor,
And then when I got tired of her, I'd shove her out the door.

To such a large degree, that's how most Americans felt about women and women workers: Use them and throw them out when you're done.

I maintained some of my connections with the labor movement during my stay in Sweden. In November 1949 I received a call from the United States. One of the kids asked whether something was wrong; it was quite extraordinary to get an international phone call in those days. The call was from Jacob Potofsky; he was asking me to attend a conference of the International Confederation of Free Trade Unions (ICFTU) in London on behalf of the American Federation of Labor (AFL). The delegate from the rubber workers union couldn't go, so there was a vacant seat. I agreed to attend as a delegate of the AFL, but I didn't expect the meeting to be so exciting, or that I would make such lasting friendships.

At the meeting I met Sigrid Ekendahl, vice president of the Swedish Labor Organization and the leading woman trade unionist in Sweden. I was the only woman from the US delegation, so I became Sigrid's roommate during the conference. She didn't speak English and I didn't speak Swedish. Oh, but we shared some beautiful moments. We spent hours sitting in bed with our English-Swedish dictionaries finding the words to talk to each other.

I was at the ICFTU convention with Walter Reuther of the CIO and Bill Green and George Meany of the AFL. There was a real focus on democracy. During this time, the tensions were growing between the Communist and non-Communist blocks in the labor movement. There was a power struggle, and the Social Democrats felt that the Communists were trying to use the organization for their own purposes. At this historic meeting, where 53 countries were represented, the ICFTU abandoned the World Federation of Free Trade Unions for being Communists. I was in favor of this split. The final manifesto said:

> Unite with us to achieve a world in which people are free from the tyranny of Communist, Fascist, Falangist, and any other form of totalitarianism, as well as from the domination and exploitation of concentrated economic power in the hands of cartels and monopolies! We reject the false theory that workers

must sacrifice political and spiritual freedom to obtain economic security and social justice.

My second important call from the United States was also from Potofsky; he called to invite me back to the US to work on the veto of the Taft-Hartley Act. The act, sponsored by Senator Robert Taft of Ohio and Representative Fred Hartley of New Jersey, reflected the decline in union political influence and the rise of business influence. The underlying philosophy of the act was to balance restrictions on employers with restrictions on unions. Denounced by unions as the "slave-labor act," the act outlawed the closed shop, jurisdictional strikes, and secondary boycotts. It also curtailed union power in emergency disputes, political contributions, and negotiated health and welfare funds. Elbert Thomas of Utah was chairman of the Labor Committee, and he refused to meet the demands of Arthur Goldberg or Phil Murray or anyone else from the labor movement. But Potofsky knew that I could get through the door because I was from Utah and I had helped get him elected. They thought I was one of very few he'd talk to. They flew me back—along with Lars, who was only about two years old—and we worked it out.

I had set up an appointment with Senator Thomas and Arthur Goldberg. The labor movement had wanted the repeal of Taft-Hartley to be the first item on the labor committee agenda, but Thomas objected. I was devastated. I wanted to talk with him about the issues until he would reach the conclusion that the act would be dangerous, but it would be his decision. I think Arthur started out too strong; I knew the most effective way to work with Thomas was to simply explain our position, without blame or expectation. I had worked with Thomas in his campaign and on the minimum wage and the extension of the Fair Labor Standards Act; I knew how he thought.

Despite our efforts, Taft-Hartley became law. It created a new legal equilibrium in the union-management relationship that was less favorable to unions.

As it turned out, it was fortunate that I was in the US to greet a delegation of Swedish visitors. A group of about a dozen of the top labor people in Sweden were visiting the US. Oliver sent word for me to meet them at LaGuardia. I was to be an informal welcoming committee; I was there as Oliver's wife, not a representative of the State Department.

When they stepped off the plane, I greeted them with *"Valkommen,"* or hearty welcome. I think they were as glad to see me as I was to see them. As they were ushered through the VIP room there was a delay. I discovered that Alex Strand, who was head of the delegation, had a card marked with a red flag, indicating that he was a socialist and should be questioned. I called the Swedish desk at the passport office and had it removed before he found out anything about it. Fortunately, I knew whom to call; it showed the importance of the interlocking relationships. We could have offended an important official.

Oliver was called away to Bonn for a meeting just before we left for our next assignment in Brussels, leaving me to close up the house, supervise the packing, and get everything to Brussels. I'll never forget our last day in Sweden—I was exhausted and overstressed. I needed someone to drive me on errands, so I asked an embassy official if I could borrow a car. He refused, strictly following the letter of the law, even though the drivers had no place else to go.

I got so frustrated, I started crying after I got off the phone. A few minutes later he called back and Karen answered the phone. She said, "Mamma can't come to the phone. She's crying." I ended up calling some Swedish friends and they came and drove me, when my own government wouldn't.

When we were leaving Sweden, the workers at the co-op gave us a going-away party and a gift. Once when visiting Gustafsberg, a co-op factory, I had met Stig Lindberg, an artist, at his studio. He asked me what I thought was beautiful. I remember feeling sort of homesick for Vermont and thinking of the beauty of the clothes I had washed hanging on the line to dry in Vermont—to me that meant comfort, home. I said, "A clothesline." He remembered this exchange, and as a going-away present, he had made a large ceramic plate with a painting of a clothesline on it. It still sits on a table in the entrance of my home in honor of our years in Sweden.

We arrived in Brussels in late 1952, but we didn't have a chance to settle in before we entered one of the most difficult times for our family. It was Christmas time, and Oliver came home with the most dejected look on his face. He told me that the ambassador called him in and told Oliver he had been brought up on charges of being a Communist.

Oliver and I had both read about the problems with the Committee on Un-American Activities back in the US, so we knew that there was a movement at home to ferret out any suspected Communists, but we never thought we were under any suspicion. Oliver's name was supposedly on Wisconsin Senator Joseph R. McCarthy's famous list of 207 card-carrying Communists in the State Department. His loyalty hearing was set for January 13, 1953.

I had never before felt so alone. We had arrived in Brussels just a few weeks before, so I had no close friends, and the people we did know we could not tell. I desperately wanted to stand by Oliver, but he had to return to the United States alone, and I had to stay with the kids in a foreign country. We told the children their father was going home on business. The ambassador told other people that Oliver had been quickly called home for consultations; he stood by Oliver throughout the ordeal.

According to the files of the FBI, "reliable informants" reported that both Oliver and I were secret members of the Communist Party for at least 13 years during the 1930s and 1940s. There was no proof of any wrongdoing, just a list of petty charges and circumstantial evidence.

One charge was that in 1940 Oliver was listed under the heading "Friends of the College" in the records of the Commonwealth College, a workers' school in Mena, Arkansas, that had been cited as a Communist organization. The reason was simple: Oliver had stayed there overnight when he was asked to visit as part of his job for the WPA's workers' education program, which trained workers to know what their rights were as part of the New Deal philosophy.

Oliver wanted to pay for his stay; they wouldn't accept his cash, so he wrote a $10 check as a contribution to the school.

Oliver's name also appeared in the 1943 mailing list of the International Publishers, which the loyalty board referred to as "the publishing agency of the Communist Party." Oliver was on the list because he had purchased *The Labor Fact Book* (cost: $1.50) to find out how the Communists slant their numbers. Again, this was part of his job, but no one considered that before bringing charges. Oliver's former boss testified on his behalf, pointing out that these activities were part of his job—his *government* job.

Few people could understand that someone could read about different political philosophies without believing them all. A few years before, when we were in Sweden, some hunters had broken into the farm in Vermont and torn the house apart. We had some left-wing magazines such as *The New Masses*, as well as some books on communism on the bookshelves there, so the hunters wrote on the walls, "Go home, Commies." The local newspaper, *The Brattleboro Reformer*, sent a reporter up to the house and he wrote a very balanced story, noting the scope of literature in our home and the fact that the comments on the walls were written by someone who was a borderline illiterate with a very narrow view of the world.

The investigators charged that Oliver was involved with a group of Communists, including Charles Kramer, Richard and Elizabeth Sasuly, and Henry H. Collins, Jr. Oliver wasn't "involved" with them; many were people I had to work with through my job at the Amalgamated. Kramer was the staff person in Senator Pepper's office handling the minimum wage bill; the Sasulys were representatives of the Food, Tobacco and Agricultural Workers Union; Collins was a labor lobbyist.

I knew that some of them were Communists, and I had even opposed their tactics. They would try to introduce bills that were so radical and impractical they could never pass. At the time, I was chair of a committee on the minimum wage that consisted of union members with the AFL and the CIO; I had been chosen to lead the group because I was accepted by both sides. As chair, I would sometimes delay votes when the Communists had enough people present to pass a measure just so that they couldn't carry a majority. I didn't want the labor movement to endorse what would become a radical bill.

They'd say that I was standing in the way of progress for poor workers and that I was a phony. I used to argue with them, "Do you want to fight or do you want to help people by working on legislation that can pass?" Both Oliver and I had contact with Communists and left-wing sympathizers in the labor movement. But these associations didn't make us party members.

Another issue that came up during the hearings involved the time that Oliver rented a room in Washington, DC, from Henry Collins, a Communist who was active on Capitol Hill. The investigators knew that there was a person who would come to meetings with Collins, and they didn't know who it was. When they found that Oliver had rented a room from Collins above a garage on St. Matthew's Court, they assumed Oliver was the man they had been looking for. They were wrong. There was no debating that we had contact with a lot of Communists through our work in the labor movement—we never did anything to hide that—but that did not make us sympathetic to the Communist cause or members of the Communist Party.

I was angry, hurt, and bitter. I couldn't imagine how anyone could make such accusations against my husband. Oliver had given his best, his energy, his youth, to his country. He was a loyal and principled person. I didn't want to keep quiet or lie about what was going on; I didn't want to accept any feeling of shame. I wanted to go public and fight it out in the open right then, but Oliver wanted to keep it quiet. Oliver felt that people wouldn't believe him. "Esther, people will say, 'Where there's smoke, there's fire.'"

Oliver was gone two or three weeks. If he had been found guilty, he would have lost his job and his professional standing. I did my best to keep going from day to day. I worked on getting the kids a good breakfast, on keeping up appearances, on getting through the next day. When I would stop to think about it, I would get angry: "Damn it, this is my country; this shouldn't be happening."

During this time, I read and reread Alan Barth's book *Loyalty of Free Men*. In it, Barth defined American heroism, and I saw my Oliver in those pages. That book kept my faith alive and helped me stay sane.

I don't think Oliver was ever quite the same after the hearings. He was calm throughout the proceedings, but he smoked his pipe constantly. He just took the arrows and let them fall off him. He had an inner strength that I didn't have, but I think the experience took its toll. Oliver developed cancer a few years later, and I have always had the feeling the cancer developed during this time of great stress. I watched him grow weaker, though I'll never know how much was due to his broken spirit and how much was due to the growing cancer.

In the end, the paperwork for Oliver's dismissal went forward to Loy Henderson, head of personnel for the State Department. We have the actual form Henderson signed; the form had two boxes, one recommending Oliver's dismissal, the other one securing his future. A single check mark secured Oliver's future. Oliver was cleared on all charges, but he would never be the same.

When Oliver returned to Brussels after the hearings, we settled into our new assignment. In addition to my traditional activities as a foreign service wife, in 1953 I helped set up the first international school for working women, modeled after the Bryn Mawr Summer School. The school, located in La Brievier, France, was organized by the ICFTU, under the auspices of the United Nations Educational, Scientific, and Cultural Organization.

The first summer session was in 1953. We brought together 50 women from 27 countries to discuss trade unionism. I didn't get along with the approach of the leadership: I wanted the sessions to be discussion-based so that the women could share and build on their experiences, but the director, Mr. Gotsfurt, wanted a traditional lecture format. Ultimately, I did two weeks my way, and he did two weeks his way. I compromised, but I didn't give in.

We had to overcome some international tensions; the war had not been over very long. When an important German trade unionist entered the lunch room, all the German women stood.

"What the hell are you doing?" I asked. They said they had to stand to show their respect. I told them not to; it was not necessary here. We were all equal.

Their formality bothered the women from The Netherlands who thought about what happened to their families during the war. One of the hardest things was to hold the school together at that moment. It was almost ready to blow apart, but we talked it out.

I survived the summer, but I didn't get involved in the school as I did at Bryn Mawr. Instead, I continued working through the ICFTU. I worked on a pamphlet titled "Women, It's Your Fight, Too," which was distributed to women in the labor movement through the ICFTU to help them get involved in the struggle against communism. It bothered me that only men were involved in the movement against the Communists; it was a women's issue, too.

Someone Oliver knew from the embassy provided me with some cartoons and information for the pamphlet. I later learned that the State Department and the CIA loved the idea of writing a pamphlet and had been slipping the cartoons to me. Most of the cartoons I didn't use because I considered them too strong. One cartoon pictured a bear pushing women down. I rejected the drawing; I resented its use of emotion instead of fact. I didn't want just to play on the Red Scare; I wanted more objective information.

In trying to get me to put the cartoons in, the man from the embassy said, "This is what women will like."

I said, "What do you know? I'm a woman."

He said, "We have experts looking at this."

I thought "To hell with you, this is my project." Oliver kept his hands out of it; he said I should do it however I wanted. In the end, the pamphlet showed how communism wasn't helping women at all; it was translated into 12 languages. That was ironic—first we were charged as Communists, then we were lauded as anti-Communist leaders.

In the summer of 1957 we returned to the United States while awaiting our next assignment. With the summer came another shock—we had lost most of our savings through a crooked real estate arrangement.

When we had lived in Washington, DC, we had bought a house in Silver Spring, Maryland. We couldn't afford to keep both that house and the farm in Vermont, so before going abroad, we sold the house to a man who ultimately swindled us out of a great deal of money. When we arrived in the US we really needed the money. The kids were entering college and we had a lot of bills. It was a terrible time. We hired an attorney and ultimately settled out of court for a fraction of what we had lost.

While we were trying to avoid financial ruin, I went with Lars to Utah to visit my 89-year-old mother who wasn't doing well, though she perked up when we arrived. Family can be a great tonic. I had assumed that we would soon be heading out for another assignment, most likely in either Australia or Montreal, so I wanted to take time to visit my family before we were gone for an extended period.

I had flown out with Lars, and the older kids drove out west on their own in a Volkswagen with a branch of tumbleweed tied to the bumper and a sign across the sides and back painted in white shoe polish: "Brussels—Utah or bust!" I stayed up late when they were to arrive because there was a tornado warning and I was concerned about the kids driving too late at night. I fell asleep, and in the morning I looked out on the porch and the kids were curled up sleeping out there. I was so happy to see them I almost woke them up to kiss them.

After getting settled in, the kids looked for work, but the only employment they could find was fruit picking—so that's what they did. They got up at 5:00AM, ate a hearty breakfast, then headed off to the orchards. They were paid 3¢ a pound for picking cherries with stems, 2¢ a pound for picking without. The same cherries sold for 80¢ to $1 a pound in the stores. The kids complained about the pay, but it was considered big pay by the Mexicans with whom they worked. They averaged 25¢ to 30¢ an hour, depending on the condition of the trees. "But," they said, "it's better than nothing." The kids told me they wanted me to go back to Washington to see that the minimum wage exemption for agricultural workers was removed or, they threatened, "We'll organize a union."

Oliver had stayed overseas a bit longer than we had. When he returned to the US he stayed in Washington, DC, to tend to some matters before reuniting with the family. Before his next assignment, he was due for a routine medical exam; that's when his doctors discovered a lump. He called and urged me to come to see him in Washington. "Esther, come on out. We've got things to decide." I argued that we could not afford the trip, but when he said, "I need you," I knew that I should be by his side. I left the kids with my mother and sister and took the first plane to Washington.

The doctors said that Oliver needed exploratory surgery. The first operation was in 1957. Oliver was diagnosed with cancer of the lymph nodes. He was given a 20% chance of survival.

I didn't know what to do. I called Utah to tell the kids. I didn't know what to say or do. I had Karen on one extension and Eric on the other. I broke down and confessed, "I don't know what to do, kids." Eric said, "Don't do a thing. You take care of Dad and we'll take care of ourselves. Don't worry about us." I'll never forget that telephone conversation. I felt so split between my husband on one side of the country and my kids on the other.

After the operation, Oliver began to feel stronger and I gathered the family together to spend some time at the farm in Vermont. In the fall, Karen and Eric returned to college, Iver went to a boarding school at Middlesex, and Lars went to school in Vermont. We stayed in Vermont through Christmas, and when winter came, Oliver, Lars, and I drove the station wagon west. We had no specific place to go, so we visited my family and Oliver's family.

After several months we returned to Washington, where we rented and later bought a house. Oliver took a job with the foreign service, managing the African desk and handling reports from all the African countries. He couldn't accept a post out of the country because of the cancer.

Our savings were gone; we had to borrow money. The kids were in private schools—Eric had a scholarship at Harvard and Karen had one at Wellesly—but money was tight. I decided to return to work as soon as possible.

The doctors could not offer any reassurance. The cancer had metastasized; the doctors couldn't understand how Oliver could stay alive. I'll never forget the day I met with the doctors and one said, "Do you know what's keeping that man alive? He is. It's a matter of will."

I don't believe we appreciate the power of the mind. Oliver received treatment at the National Institutes of Health in Bethesda, Maryland, and they were intrigued by his case. They tried a lot of new things on him. He never regained his previous strength, but he still loved to work on the farm in Vermont. I watched his body grow somewhat stronger, but the cancer was still there. We continued to live in the shadow of doubt—and would for 20 years more.

Chapter 6

"Esther, Where Have You Been?"

Before leaving for Sweden, the Amalgamated had given me a great farewell party and the gift of an alligator bag. (Today, my grandchildren would yell about using animal hides, but in those days it was considered a rare and elegant gift—a sign that I was moving up in the world.) At the party, Jacob Potofsky had urged me not to stay away too long. Ten years later I was back.

When we were settled in Washington, DC, and ready to get to work, I met with Potofsky and Frank Rosenbloom, secretary-treasurer and the second in command at the Amalgamated, to talk about coming back to work for the union. Frank and I never got along very well because he wanted to control everything. One day he stormed into my office waving a letter in his hand; he had come to Washington from Chicago just to lace me down about a letter I had sent someone from his district. He scolded me every time I did anything on my own, but in the end I went my own way. I was careful. I just stopped putting things in writing to people in his district.

At the meeting to discuss coming back to work for the union, Frank sneered and said condescendingly, "What's the matter, Esther, can't you get a job? Do we have to give you a job again?"

"You certainly do not," I responded, ready to storm out. I had helped them no end; Hillman and Potofsky had relied on me heavily. I was furious. Potofsky smoothed things over. He said, "Don't worry Esther, we'll work things out."

Potofsky arranged for Jim Carey of the electrical workers, who was also the president of the Industrial Union Department of the AFL-CIO, to give me a call. I could do the same lobbying work for the Industrial Union Department, of which the Amalgamated was a part. I did the same work, but my paycheck came from the Industrial Union Department rather than the Amalgamated, and I was out from under Frank's thumb.

When we discussed the terms of my employment, Carey asked me to accept a salary that was $2,000 less than that of the man who held the job before, even though the job was identical. He had the audacity to say, "Oh, Esther, you don't need the money. Oliver has a good job."

I was appalled. I asked, "Is that the way you negotiate for all your people in the union?" That was my first direct experience with equal pay issues—and it was for myself. Eventually, Carey agreed to pay me the full salary, and I began lobbying for the Industrial Union Department.

Those early days with the Industrial Union Department reminded me of breaking ground as a woman lobbyist before I left for Sweden in 1948. By the time I got back from overseas 10 years later, Kennedy was in the Senate. (So much for the lobbyists who said he wouldn't amount to much.)

Shortly after returning from Brussels, I was walking down the hall in the Senate office building and heard, "Esther, Esther. Where have you been? I've missed you." The voice had a strong New England accent.

I turned and there stood John F. Kennedy.

Not too long after that I bumped into Ralph Dungan, one of Kennedy's top aides, in the hallway. He invited me to stop by his office, where he told me that Kennedy was preparing to make his bid for the presidency. They wanted me to work on the campaign; they were aware that I knew people in Utah, in addition to my contacts in the labor movement.

When I told Potofsky I supported Kennedy, he warned me not to stick my neck out until the other labor leaders made their decision of whom to support.

"But now is when he needs your support," I responded.

I didn't wait. I trusted my gut feelings and did what I wanted to do. I think that's one of the reasons Kennedy respected me. I joined him independently, before the rest of the labor people followed. Potofsky wasn't pleased with my decision, but he saw that I felt very strongly about Kennedy.

Kennedy's people invited me to a working lunch in Jack's office. At mealtime, Jacqueline Kennedy had food sent up: meat loaf, peas, mashed potatoes, milk, and fruit for dessert. We discussed how best to get labor involved in the campaign and who should be the head of the labor desk. After lunch, Kennedy's people brought out three-by-five cards, each listing a Utah delegate to the Democratic Convention. The cards listed details on each delegate's habits and likes and dislikes; where that person went to church, the names of their spouses and children. In Utah it was critical to get the Mormon vote, and because I knew many of the delegates already, I was to review those cards and think of ways to move people into the Kennedy camp. I got a lot of help from my sister, Algie Ballif, who was a leader of the Democratic Party in Utah; she knew most of the people whom I didn't know.

We spent the afternoon going over the cards, and I agreed to help work the campaign in Utah. I spent my time working on the Kennedy campaign, but I was still officially employed by the union. Nowadays, you're not allowed to have campaign workers paid by other organizations. I went to Utah and met with the head of the Democratic Party in Utah on Kennedy's behalf. He wasn't eager to talk to me; he even went as far as saying, "You people from Washington don't understand Utah."

He didn't recognize my married name, so finally one of the Democratic bigwigs who knew my sister told him that I was Esther Eggertsen, born and raised in Provo and a graduate of Brigham Young University. He laughed; then he listened.

Back in Washington, Arthur Goldberg and I handled most of the work on the labor desk at the Democratic Party national headquarters. I sat at a phone and talked to district campaign workers around the country and made sure they got the pamphlets, bumper stickers, and other material we were putting out. I made sure I knew when union locals were meeting, and I sent telegrams from Kennedy to the locals so that someone could stand up and read it along with the other announcements. I had people in the field calling me to tell me about the concerns in their areas. We had a network. I heard that some farmers in the northern Rockies were worried about the railroads closing grain elevators, and we got a message to their meeting that Kennedy was aware of the problem and would look into it if elected president. I think the telegram technique was one of the best campaign tools we had. I had so many calls going out all over the country that I had three separate phones on my desk! In those days we didn't have a single phone that could handle multiple phone lines.

Bobby Kennedy walked by my desk one frantic day and innocently asked how things were going. "Terrible," I shot back, complaining that I could get nothing done when there was so little cooperation among the workers. I then unloaded about my day of frustrations and miscommunications; I named names and laid the blame where I thought it belonged. He grabbed my wrists and walked from desk to desk, gathering my coworkers. He sat us all down in his office and said, "Esther, now tell them what you told me." We had it out—I was wrong on some issues and my coworkers were wrong on others—but the experience taught me to have my facts straight before complaining. I call this the Bobby Kennedy technique, and I have used it myself over and over.

By the time the convention started—and after a great deal of work—the Utah delegates were in Kennedy's corner. I wanted Utah to be the state to put Kennedy over the top, but it didn't happen; I think it was the Wyoming delegates who clinched the Kennedy nomination.

After Kennedy was elected, I was asked, "What do you want?"

I had assumed that after the election I would return to my job with the union. I wasn't working for Kennedy so that I could get a job. I've always hated the jobs-for-the-boys thinking.

I thought about it, then said, "The Women's Bureau." I had a base in the labor movement and I understood the needs of working women. I was comfortable there.

Ralph Dungan asked me about accepting a post at the United Nations. I was tempted, but I didn't feel up to the challenge. I didn't feel competent with international issues, and more important, Oliver was sick and needed me.

The Women's Bureau had come to mind because I had worked with them in the past. The Women's Bureau in the Department of Labor had been established in 1920 to do studies to find out what was happening to women in the readjustment period after World War I. The formal mandate was "to formulate standards and policies which shall promote the welfare of wage-earning women, improve their working conditions, increase their efficiency, and advance their opportunities for profitable employment."

The bureau devoted a great deal of time to documenting the abysmal working conditions of women in the canneries, the laundries, the cotton mills, the garment factories—those places where work was available to women. In the early days of the bureau a lot of changes were taking place in the workforce, and women were slowly gaining certain political rights. Remember, 1920 was the first year women had the right to vote; they were still largely resigned to the shadows of political life.

Ironically, the very organization that was dedicated to improving women's wages and working conditions capped the salaries of most Women's Bureau employees. Utah Senator Reed Smoot insisted on a proviso in the appropriations bill stating that only two people on the staff could be paid more than $2,000 a year, a considerable sum in those days. But what was disturbing was the remark that followed: "No woman on earth is worth more than that."

While less obvious, such prejudice against women continued well into the Kennedy years. Shortly after I was appointed, Arthur Goldberg organized a big luncheon for all the ranking incoming Democrats and the outgoing Republicans at the Labor Department. By rank, that luncheon should have included two women—Alice Leopold, the outgoing Women's Bureau head, and me as her replacement. Before the lunch, Arthur called and said that some of the officials didn't want Alice along for some reason;

would I mind taking her to lunch at Rive Gauche while the men got together somewhere else? Like a fool, I did it. I suppose I was expected to be grateful he said he'd pick up the tab.

I have always had a lot of respect for the first director of the bureau, Mary Anderson, who came to America from Sweden in 1889 when she was 16. By age 22 she was a skilled shoeworker and president of the Stitchers Local 94. She was an inspiration to me; she respected workers and devoted her life to improving their working conditions. She spoke in broken English and made a lot of grammatical errors. This bothered some people who felt it was inappropriate to have a representative of government who couldn't speak "proper" English, but the working people understood her. She really knew what she was talking about. She was honest. She wasn't a bureaucrat. She was a worker. She gave working women a voice in government.

When I took over the Women's Bureau, I wanted to make some changes to bring back the spirit of the bureau in the days of Mary Anderson and her successor Frieda Miller, to revive it from its fallow years under Eisenhower. I wanted to focus more energy on low-income women working in factories and service workers rather than exclusively the concerns of professional women working in offices and white-collar jobs. From its beginning, the bureau had been subject to friction between women, largely along class lines. For too long, I fear, the Women's Bureau seemed to regard its mission as one of helping women who were educated, middle class, and usually White. I felt that if resources were tight—as they always are in government—and if time is scarce—as it always is in life—then surely the biggest part of the effort should go to help those women who need help most.

I met with my staff at the Women's Bureau when I accepted the job, and I discussed with them my intentions to make some changes. Many people at the bureau didn't want any change; they wanted to hold onto every part of their jobs, to control their little fiefdoms. One of the high-ranking staff members had strong objections to the proposed changes.

"I'm the director," I had to remind her.

"Yes, but I'll be here long after you're gone," she responded. She basically admitted that she and the other workers would pay me lip service, but that when circumstances change—and they always do—then I would be out. That's how the Washington bureaucracy works.

I did a lot of speaking when I was at the Women's Bureau. At a large high school in Los Angeles, I spoke to a huge auditorium full of girls about the importance of getting an education and learning a skill. I told the girls that most of them were going to have to work.

"How many of you think you'll have a home and kids and a family?" I asked. Hands went up all over.

"How many of you want to work?" One or two hands went up.

"How many of your mothers work?" All of those hands went up again.

"Do you think your life is going to be that different from your mother's? If you must work, don't you want a decent job? Do you want to do the low-paying work that your mother is doing?"

A lot of students came to me afterward and said they were concerned because they saw the truth in my message. In those days, nine out of 10 girls would work outside the home at some point in their lives, but each of the girls thought that she would be that 10th girl.

My challenge was to let these girls know that they should be ready to support their families, as nearly 2.5 million women did in 1963. And even if they didn't enter the workforce out of financial necessity, girls at that time would have raised their families by age 35 or 40 and they probably would have 35 or 40 more years of productive life; they would be unprepared to make the most of those years if they didn't have a good education.

All in all, I had a lot of hostile feedback for taking a stand in favor of preparing girls for the reality of the world of work. One of the nasty cartoons that was done about me showed me driving women out of the home and into the factories. It was really very misleading. I wasn't pushing women into the workforce; women were already there. In 1960 women made up 33% of the nation's labor force, although nearly 80% of those women worked in stereotypical women's jobs, such as clerical work, teaching, and nursing.

To deal with some of these questions, I ran a series of four regional conferences for working women. I wanted to understand their concerns. At the conference in Michigan, a group of housewives came in. They asked why there wasn't any economic value assigned to the work they did, staying home taking care of the house and kids. They ended up standing in the back of the room chanting, "We want to be part of the GNP."

I tried to tell women who defined themselves as "just housewives" that they were much more than that. For one thing, I quarreled with the term "housewife." These women were not married to their houses; they were homemakers. Homemakers were not listed as part of the labor force, but they actually made up the largest single occupational group in the early 1960s. Thirty years have passed, and we still have a long way to go to value child care and home care.

Minority women faced unique problems because they were denied opportunities because of their race and gender. When attending one of the regional conferences, I spoke briefly to a Black woman who was cleaning the toilets in the hotel. As it turns out, she had a master's degree, but the only job she could get was cleaning toilets. Such prejudice is a tragic waste of talent.

On another trip I traveled out to Arizona to speak to some migrant farmworkers who were living in a shack out behind a fancy stable for race horses. I was appalled not only by the poor conditions of the workers, but by the fact that those horses were treated better than the humans.

Some of the most heated debates at the conference involved the complicated issues surrounding protective legislation, particularly the delicate balance between protection and overprotection. Some states passed laws designed to protect working women—such as laws limiting the weight they could lift or the hours they could work—but by definition this disqualified certain women for certain jobs. For example, laws against night work could keep female nurses from accepting work on certain shifts; laws prohibiting a woman from lifting a 50-pound box might exclude her from certain factory work. In one case I heard about a woman who was lifting a load on an assembly line; when asked about why she was doing the work for her coworker in violation of the weight restriction, she said, "He couldn't lift it, so I did." That woman was paid 15¢ less per hour than her male coworker.

We also worked on wage issues. I'll never forget trying to get the professional women to help get the domestic workers covered under the Fair Labor Standards Act. Oh no, the white-collar women wanted cheap labor to work in their homes while they went to the office. I tried to show the white-collar women in good-paying jobs that they would benefit by helping create minimum standards for all working women.

Our office created an Equal Pay Committee and discussed the impact of minimum wages. I think the professional women eventually saw that by paying lower wages to the women who worked for them, they also kept wages low for themselves. It lowered women's worth everywhere. Even today there appears to be a virtual conspiracy among some professional women to keep a supply of low-wage labor. Too many women themselves put low economic value on child care and housekeeping, indicating that they falsely believe that this kind of work isn't "worth" much.

So many women had to overcome the false impression that they were working for "pin money." I heard testimony on the minimum wage when a working woman was asked whether her earnings were pin money. Distressed, she responded, "Well, if it's pin money, then it's the pins that hold my family together."

It was difficult for some people to realize that millions of women were working out of economic necessity. In 1964 the 4 million women who were heads of their households weren't working for pin money. The 655,000 mothers with small children whose husbands made less than $3,000 a year weren't working for pin money. The migrant mother who carried her child with her to the hot fields to earn less than $1 an hour wasn't working for pin money. These women weren't working for vacation money or special indulgences; they were working because their families needed the money.

I traveled around the country holding hearings on equal pay. During a roundtable discussion in Los Angeles, the women raised a number of concerns. We heard, "We're concerned about equal pay." "We're concerned about advancement in our jobs." "We're concerned that we can't become tenured professors." I had to ask an agricultural worker, "What is your greatest need?"

"Toilets," she responded. There was absolute silence. It was terrific. Afterward the women were talking and the agricultural workers confessed, "Do you know that sometimes you have pee on your lettuce?" That woman wasn't concerned with job advancement—today's "glass ceiling"—she wanted a restroom away from the dirt and leering men. That episode helped us in our fight to get sanitary facilities in the fields for the agricultural workers. It enlarged the coalition in favor of reform. Things start from the bottom up.

As my work in the Women's Bureau so often reminded me, we desperately needed a study of where women were in society. We needed a baseline so that we could figure out where we needed to go. How many women stayed home to raise their children? How many worked outside the home? What were they paid? We couldn't call the increase in the number of working women "progress," because not everyone considered it progress to have more women in the workforce. But we could all agree that it would be progress for working women to get a fair wage and decent working conditions.

I moved on the idea of a President's Commission on the Status of Women soon after Kennedy was elected. The time was right for a women's commission, and I knew that if Kennedy didn't take the lead on women's issues, then Lyndon Baines Johnson (LBJ) might. LBJ and I had had our differences over the years because I had supported Kennedy for president, but I had admired him greatly. Shortly after the election, I went to LBJ's office in a kiss-and-make-up meeting, and LBJ escorted me to the elevator.

"Esther, what are you going to do for women?" he asked. It was clear to me that Johnson had recognized an important political constituency—women. He was shrewd that way; he knew politics.

It wasn't a new idea. The concept of a commission on the status of women was first floated back at the end of World War II, when Rosie the Riveter and other working women gave up their jobs for the returning men. Representative Emmanuel Cellars of Brooklyn had introduced legislation calling for a congressional commission on the legal status of women annually throughout the 1950s, but he never got to first base. His idea was to use the approach that President Truman had used in his Civil Rights Commission's landmark study on the status of American Blacks, "To Secure These Rights." The text of the report could almost remain the same with the substitution of the word "women" for "Negro."

I envisioned a President's Commission on the Status of Women that would compile a report measuring the life and conditions of working women, as well as a blueprint for change. I wanted to have a series of roundtable discussions across the country to hammer out recommendations for reform.

Such a commission would also help to deflect the renewed drive for passage of the Equal Rights Amendment (ERA) to the Constitution. I opposed the ERA at that time, as did many in the labor movement, because it could have removed special protections of women workers, such as state minimum wage laws that applied to women only. I didn't think the ERA would be a cure-all, and I recognized its potential to harm working women. The critical question—one that remains relevant today—is: Are women better off being singled out for protection, or are they better served by erasing all legal distinctions between women and men? As the lettuce pickers and the cafeteria workers know, it depends on your status.

The most important examples involved minimum wage laws. Ever since the first national minimum wage of 25¢ an hour was passed in 1938, its reach had generally been limited to industries with strong unions and mostly male employees. Employers had successfully prevented the extension of minimum wage protection to the workers who needed it most—the laundry workers, hotel and restaurant workers, domestics, and low-level food processors. Most of these were women's jobs; they tended to be unskilled positions, especially subject to exploitation. In the late 19th century the four most common women's occupations were, in order, factory work, domestic service, secretarial and clerical work, and teaching; in 1960 the occupations were the same, but the order had changed: factory work, secretarial and clerical work, teaching, and domestic service.

Women working in these largely unskilled jobs faced exploitation. They had limited opportunities for training or advancement; these were the only jobs they could get. "Don't you think 50¢ an hour is enough for scrubbing floors on your hands and knees? You're free to quit."

"Your bus was late? I'll find someone who lives closer to work."

"You don't want to work late because your baby needs to nurse? Maybe you shouldn't be working at all."

These are not exaggerations. One evening in a hotel corridor I passed a scrubwoman on her knees. The front of her dress was wet and dark; her breasts were swollen and overflowing with milk. I asked if I could help and she said, "No, I need this job."

To protect workers such as these, a number of states had passed minimum wages for women only in certain jobs. I supported minimums for all workers—men and women—but the fact was that most state industrial boards preferred to think of women as the weaker sex and were willing to offer them a minimum wage, but not their husbands and brothers. In fact, a state court in Washington threw out a minimum wage law for both sexes on the grounds that it violated the 14th Amendment "right to contract." The employers argued that if a man wanted to work for less, who should stop him? But, said the court, society did have to protect women and motherhood, so the law could apply to women.

To me, half a loaf was better than none. And, after all, minimum wages for women helped push men's wages up, too. A bellhop at the Wiltshire Hotel in Los Angles thanked me for my work on the minimum wage. He had heard me on the radio, and he said he got a raise because the law gave a minimum wage for women. After all, you couldn't pay a man less than a woman!

Plenty of women objected to any statutory distinctions between women and men and supported the ERA. Many of these women came from the National Women's Party, an outgrowth of the old women's suffrage movement. I found it frustrating because so many of these ardent feminists came from good families and held good jobs, if they worked at all, and they had not the slightest idea of the problems their sisters faced at the other end of the social and economic scale. They wanted a symbolic emancipation from male expectations of womanhood, but most of them did nothing to help support us with the bread-and-butter issues such as minimum wages that millions of the invisible women depended on. I considered these elite, privileged old ladies members of "The Old Frontier." I knew I was on the right side when I noticed that the same people who fought us on extending the Fair Labor Standards Act were vigorously supporting the ERA. If my enemies were supporting the ERA, then my fears must have been well founded.

I became identified with opposition to the ERA. The amendment had been up for votes in the Senate, but each time it failed to get the needed two-thirds vote. When the ERA supporters would besiege Carl Hayden, the old Arizona Democrat and chairman of the Senate Judiciary Committee, he would call me and say, "Esther, the tennis-shoe ladies are here again," referring to the stuffy, old conservatives. "What do I tell them?"

What he said was that he would not let an ERA bill out of his committee without the famous Hayden rider, an amendment declaring that nothing in the ERA could be used to upset special state laws governing women already in the workforce. It became known as the "killer amendment," because unless the states gave up protecting women, the conservatives didn't want the bill. In those days, the ERA was a most definitely conservative issue. Kennedy favored the amendment only with the Hayden rider to preserve protective legislation for women.

Of course, I knew that laws to protect women could also be laws that kept women subordinate to men. That's why the President's Commission on the Status of Women was intended to come up with recommendations to achieve equal rights for women in all the places they needed reinforcement, without resorting to the ERA. This "specific bills for specific ills" approach was the one I favored.

On December 14, 1961, Kennedy signed the Executive Order 10980 establishing the President's Commission on the Status of Women. Its mission: to examine the treatment of women under all laws and customs and to make recommendations for federal and state action to achieve equality. There was a lot of talk about the importance of family values and how women working outside the home undermined those values. We carefully combined references to a woman's sacred duty to the American family with language affirming her right to make her own way. Remember, at that time, feminism was commonly considered an antiquated and ridiculous notion. Strong women were accused of being "unwomanly" or "mannish"—or they were discounted as being "just like a woman."

After we had drawn up the executive order, I realized we hadn't said anything about funding, so Arthur Goldberg, always the lawyer, took a pen and wrote in, "Members of the Commission, except those receiving other compensation from the United States, shall receive such compensation as the President shall fix in a manner to be hereafter determined." Then I personally ran around to all the cabinet departments that had something to do with women at work and in society and got their signatures of endorsement and scrounged staff workers and raised about $250,000 to pay our expenses.

Arthur Goldberg and I put the commission together, and we were careful to pick 11 men and 15 women who represented a broad spectrum of both experience and thought. I was executive vice chair and Eleanor Roosevelt was chair. I had wanted Eleanor Roosevelt appointed to give the commission the highest status, but Kennedy still carried a grudge against her for her support of Adlai Stevenson. Kennedy wasn't willing to ask her to serve, but he welcomed her participation if she would serve. I asked her, and she agreed. When Mrs. Roosevelt died just before the commission issued the final report, Kennedy's admiration for her led him to announce that he would leave her chair open. "There could be no suitable replacement."

We had a lot of trouble with the women and women's groups that wanted to be involved with the commission. I bent over backwards to keep the commission politically and geographically balanced. The goal was to create a commission that consisted of members of the power structure, people who could affect change; I didn't want the commission to become just another political plum. We had representatives from industry, academe, Blacks, professional women, religious groups, and both houses of Congress; we tried to select umbrella groups that represented the big power blocks. We wanted to avoid the garden clubs and the women's divisions of the Democratic and Republican Parties.

Some people just didn't understand why certain members were selected for the commission; for instance, India Edwards, the only woman member of the Democratic National Committee, was very difficult. She wanted to be on the commission—she felt she deserved to be—but I didn't want it to become a political reward for administration supporters. Frankly, she was angry that I got the jobs that she wanted. She used to say, "They think Esther is the only one who knows about women; they give her everything." What India seemed to forget was that she had supported Johnson and campaigned against Kennedy in the presidential primaries. It was she who spread the gossip during the election that Kennedy had Addison's disease and required cortisone injections. He did, but it had no bearing on his ability to serve as president.

We also had a problem with a woman put forward by LBJ. He had insisted that the commission include Ellen Boddy of Texas, a wealthy ranchowner who had been a big contributor to his campaign. I didn't want to appoint her—I felt that she represented no constituency—but it wasn't worth the fight; we had to keep LBJ happy.

At the first commission meeting, Mrs. Boddy asked some of the most basic questions. She didn't seem to understand anything: "Minimum wage? What do you mean about minimum wage? You mean you have laws about that?"

We had a big reception at LBJ's home the night of the first meeting. In the car on the way there, Mrs. Roosevelt asked me, "Why did you appoint her to the commission?"

I explained that the appointment was a favor to LBJ. When we got to LBJ's home, I stood next to Mrs. Roosevelt in the receiving line. When Mrs. Boddy came through the line, I heard Mrs. Roosevelt say in LBJ's ear, "That's Mrs. Boddy. I wonder where she came from? She doesn't seem to know about anything."

Later, when we drove back to the hotel, I said to her, "I was surprised at your remark about Mrs. Boddy."

She said, "I didn't look at you, Mrs. Peterson. I was afraid I would have smiled."

Eleanor Roosevelt had a beautiful way of letting people know what she thought. And, as it turned out, Mrs. Boddy was wonderful at helping us keep our feet on the ground. We always had to think in terms of writing the report in such a way that the average person would understand it. In the end, Ellen Boddy became our "representative of the people."

Mrs. Roosevelt contributed to the commission up to her final days. During one meeting at Hyde Park she looked very tired. She sat through the meeting with her eyes closed. I thought: "Oh dear, she's sleeping." Then we came to a very difficult point and she sat up and made a statement that brought the entire discussion into focus. She had been listening to everything and absorbing it.

When we submitted the final report, I believe we had assembled a complete statistical and narrative snapshot of the status of American women. I wanted the study to present the facts, which meant a lot of statistics. The role of women in society was too emotional a topic to deal with in any other way. I knew that as soon as we would get into editorializing, we'd be in trouble. We had to practice the art of the possible.

The report was in eight parts. The first, titled "An Invitation to Action," spelled out the facts: the lives of women were unalterably changing. Women were living longer and going farther in school and the workplace, but still suffered the limitations of discrimination and unequal pay.

The section discussing women and employment included a chart titled "Most Women in Federal Service Are in Lower Grades." It showed that most women worked in grade three and four jobs, which paid $3,760 to $4,985. Very few women worked in the top grades—15 to 18—which brought in salaries of $13,730 to $18,500. In fact, an embarrassingly low 1.4% of the top posts were held by women. That chart really showed how most women were stuck in the low-paying jobs.

The commission also took on the tough fight over the right to birth control and information on sex. It's hard to believe that this would amount to any kind of fight, but birth control was considered a dangerous topic then. Too many commission members didn't want to get involved in the issue of sexual freedom; "Oh, do we need to go into that?" was the typical response. I had a tough balancing act to do. Some people didn't want the word "sex" to appear; others wanted to make sure the word "family" did appear; still others wanted to advocate access to legal abortion. Keep in mind, Massachusetts and Connecticut still banned the sale of contraceptives.

In the end, we agreed that we would not make the point in the same bold typeface as the other recommendations. The text read, in its entirety: "Women should have opportunity for education about sex and human reproduction in the context of education for family life." Despite its modesty, these tepid words were the first in any government report to urge that women had the right to information about birth control. This was the most difficult of all the recommendations to get accepted.

In other cases our topics remain surprisingly contemporary. For instance, we also argued that the lack of day care for children of working parents was putting the brakes on economic expansion and women's work opportunities. Some people feared that endorsing day care would encourage women to work outside the home, never mind that many women had no choice. Others argued that the lack of adequate day care contributed to the decay of the family because children were left alone after school. Again, we let the facts speak for themselves, showing that latchkey children were returning from school to empty houses because their mothers were away working.

On equal pay the commission took a firm stand: equal pay for equal work. The need for this had been plain for years, and it was driven home at a commission hearing in Salt Lake City (we eventually took testimony from citizens in 40 states). In Salt Lake I visited the great Mormon Church-owned Zion's Cooperative Mercantile Institute, where I spoke to women in the china department. These women had to take extensive training on china, crystal, and silverware so they could provide top-notch service to their customers. But, simply because they were women, they were paid $15 per week less than the untrained college boys in the sporting goods department who sold footballs and catcher's mitts. That hit me hard.

As it happened, equal pay was one of our first victories. Even before the commission report was published, the 1963 Equal Pay Amendment to the Fair Labor Standards Act was passed by Congress and signed by the president. It was an important victory, even though it wasn't as strong a measure as we would have liked. We lost on comparability; how do you compare the economic value of a nurse with a garbage collector? We favored a study on the issue; after all, it is one of the reasons women, on average, are paid less than men.

We also agitated against employment discrimination in government hiring. We checked into the history and found that when the Civil Service Act was passed, the promotion system was based on merit. In 1864, when women were first entering government work, Congress established a top salary for female clerks of $600 a year; male clerks earned $1,200 to $1,800 a year. As it happened, the female clerks were so much more efficient than many of the male clerks that a civil service equal pay bill was passed by Congress in 1870, allowing the government to pay women the same as men, if it was felt that the women performed the same work. All we did was extend this to the public sector.

In 1934, during the Great Depression when male breadwinners needed work, the US attorney general ruled that employment offices could specify men or women for a job. Of course, 94% of the highest paid jobs were "men only" listings.

We thought it was time to revisit the issue, so the commission asked Attorney General Robert Kennedy to review the practice and render a new opinion. We were having a commission meeting at Hyde Park, the Roosevelt estate, when we learned that the attorney general ruled that the president had the right to forbid job selection by sex in the civil service. The president promptly responded with a directive to all federal agencies requiring that they make all job selections—hiring, firing, promotion, and training—without regard to sex, except in a few unusual circumstances justified by the Civil Service Commission, such as jobs requiring the use of firearms. When employers called state employment offices with a job opening they could no longer say "I want a man," or "This is a woman's job." Shortly afterward, I sat in a public employment office to see how things were going. When the phone rang, the caller asked for a man for a certain job. Because I was in the room, the employment director said, "You can't say that anymore. Just give me a job description and I'll send the best person for the job." The reply came: "Well, if you can't send me a man, then for hell's sake, send a *good* woman!"

In the section on women under the law, we lamented the fact that three states—South Carolina, Alabama, and Mississippi—still did not allow women to sit on state juries. It had taken a 1957 civil rights act to gain the right for women to sit on federal juries. In 26 other states, women could excuse themselves from jury duty because of their "delicate and sheltered" nature.

We also took up the issue of property rights for married women. Some states prevented women from direct inheritance; others stated that a married woman could not go into business for herself without permission from the court. In four states, a man had complete control over his wife's earnings. These laws have been done away with since the commission called attention to them.

For health care, we argued for prenatal attention for women and counseling for uneducated young mothers. We included a chapter on volunteer work, though there was debate over whether it gave employers the idea that women didn't really care about money. We ended up with a recommendation that volunteer work be officially encouraged, and that this "experience credit" should count as a plus in hiring evaluations.

We included a strong recommendation for continuing education programs for adults since more and more people, especially women, were changing careers or just starting to work. Mary Bunting, president of Radcliffe College (we called her Polly), pushed hard for this foresightful recommendation. We encouraged women to go back to work and school rather than face an empty nest.

On the ERA question, we ultimately settled on a carefully worded compromise. I had been careful to appoint Marguerite Rawalt of the National Federation of Business and Professional Women's Clubs, an ardent ERA supporter, to the commission. I knew the battle was inevitable and that we would have to sit down with our opponents. The report stated first that equal rights for all persons is basic to democracy and must be reflected in the law of the land. But we argued that the principle of equality was embodied in the Fifth and 14th Amendments to the Constitution and that a separate Equal Rights Amendment was not necessary. We wanted a case to go before the US Supreme Court to clarify the issue. I strongly believed that specific legislation targeting specific problems—specific bills for specific ills—was a far more effective way of getting focused results and reforms than a one-sentence addition to the Constitution. But we did note that if the problems persisted after judicial clarification, we would consider the amendment.

On October 11, 1963—Eleanor Roosevelt's birthday—the president accepted our report, *American Women: An Invitation to Action*, with graciousness and praise. The publication became a Government Printing Office bestseller; it was later published by Scribner's, with an introduction written by noted anthropologist Margaret Mead. Copies of the report went out to forums and seminars on women's issues, as well as to interested people who called or wrote. Our embassies overseas distributed the report around the world; it was even translated into Japanese. I sent one of the Japanese editions to LBJ with a card: "Here's a little bedtime reading." He wrote back, "It's fine, Esther, but are you sure they translated it correctly?"

The President's Commission laid the groundwork for the creation of the National Women's Committee on Civil Rights. It seemed that within the civil rights movement the voices of Black women were rarely heard. There was a great potential force we could tap into if we could motivate the women. Women are important in shaping public opinion and needed to be recognized as such.

Just before the president flew to Berlin for his great "Ich Bin ein Berliner" speech, he had been drawing up a voting rights bill. I took it on myself to object that the White House had not brought any women in on the deliberations with outside civic organizations. Evidently, the message got through because I got a message from Ralph Dungan encouraging me to organize a meeting for women. That was one pleasure of working with Jack: present him with a good idea and he would respond to it quickly.

We had 10 days to coordinate a meeting with leading Black and White women interested in civil rights. We invited representatives of both Black and White women's organizations to Washington to discuss how we could get more involved in the civil rights movement. In the end, the National Women's Committee on Civil Rights consisted of 300 female leaders representing 50 million women. This group had tremendous potential for developing understanding and influencing public opinion.

I called a quick planning meeting of women interested in the issue in my office; that was the first time some of the White club women had sat down with Black women in the same room for conversation. It was a new experience for some of them; often we live so far apart it's as though we're living in different worlds. Too often different groups of people never bother to talk to one another or to share ideas. After the meeting, one of the White women said, "I had no idea they had so many different ideas among themselves." Some of the women had assumed that the Blacks would be monolithic and speak with one voice.

Our first meeting was at the White House. Right away the fur started to fly over who would be chair. The Blacks wanted a Black chair; the Whites wanted a White chair. The battle reminded me of my old days in the garment industry, trying to get the Jews and the

Italians to work together. Ultimately, we selected two cochairs of the committee: Patricia Roberts Harris, a Black woman who led the Negro sorority Delta Sigma Theta and who later became secretary of Health, Education, and Welfare; and General Mildred McAfee Horton, a White woman who was head of the Women's Navy Corps.

We came up with a four-point program: Take a Step (start talking about racial problems in your community), Take a Stand (adopt a plan of action), Take a Part (speak up, get involved), and Take a Share (wear a button and donate money to organizations that support this mission). We also came up with the idea for the Take a Hand project; we wanted to have White women come into the Black communities in the South and walk to school with Black children during integration. We didn't get very far with it; few women had the courage to do it.

At the end of the meeting, I stood next to Dorothy Height and said, "Dorothy, today I wish I were Black." I felt that if I were Black, I could do something to really make a difference.

She said, "Esther, if you were Black, you'd never have this job." It struck me that she was right. I could support racial equality emotionally and politically—and I did—but being White, there were limits to what I could do. What we really needed was genuine equality of opportunity.

The Commission on the Status of Women had recognized that rigid application of labor standards limiting hours, night work, and weights that women would lift could exclude women from some jobs. So when the Civil Rights Act of 1964 was passed with Title VII prohibiting sex discrimination in employment, I was taken aback. I was on the record opposing Title VII primarily because I was afraid that the sex amendment—which had been proposed by Representative Howard Smith of Virginia, an outspoken opponent of Civil Rights—was just an attempt to defeat the Civil Rights bill. I didn't want anything to jeopardize the Civil Rights Act. It seems the ploy backfired; instead of holding minorities back, the bill moved women forward. I had been wrong.

In the summer of 1963 I got a telephone call from John Leslie, information officer for the Labor Department, notifying me that Arthur Goldberg was planning to name me assistant secretary of labor for Labor Standards. This new position made me the highest ranking woman in the Kennedy administration. The idea still hadn't hit me. The responsibility was immense: I was to oversee the Bureau of Labor Standards and to handle labor issues, such as minimum wage, workers' compensation, hours, and health and safety protections.

My appointment and the creation of a new assistant secretary post had to be approved by Congress. Some of the legislators weren't up to speed on my nomination and the word went around the floor, "Vote for Esther." Afterward, I was told that some Congress members said, "Esther Peterson? Oh, I thought I was voting for Esther Van Wagoner Tufty." Tufty was a well-known Washington reporter.

As assistant secretary, I was very concerned about how much money we were paying in workers' compensation for federal employees. There were many accidents reported by federal employees, especially mail carriers, who drove automobiles. When government workers were injured in these accidents, they collected workers' compensation. I also received letters from employees asking why they had to wait so long to get their compensation checks. I wanted to find out why the system was so slow, but I couldn't get an answer within the bureau, so I hired a nongovernment outfit to do an independent study of the worker's compensation system. I'll never forget that one company I interviewed asked me, "How do you want the results to come out?" Needless to say, they didn't get the contract. In time, we had the bureaucratic glitches in the system worked out, and we did it all in-house.

I was also very concerned about occupational accidents. In 1968 industrial accidents killed 14,500 people, disabled 2 million, and injured 7 million more. Many of these incidents were avoidable, but life and limb were considered the price of progress. Though the bill didn't pass until after I left office, we did the early work on creating the Occupational Safety and Health Administration (OSHA), which established federal safety and health standards.

As part of our efforts, the Labor Department prepared a brochure on workplace safety titled "On the Job Slaughter: A National Shame." On the cover was a picture of a man riding on a forklift in a big warehouse; the man had been decapitated when a box dropped on him. During the hearings on the creation of OSHA, I was accused of misrepresenting the issue because the picture was three years old. It was, but I argued that the same machines were still in use. A few days after the brochure was released, there was an accident just like the one in the picture. It was tragic but it proved my point. In this country, it often takes a tragedy for us to wake up and take notice.

As assistant secretary for Labor Standards, I did a lot of work on minimum wage laws, but every time we attempted to expand the number of people covered by the minimum wage laws, the employers tried to find ways to side-step the requirements. In one case, the labor laws had exemptions for people in executive positions, so the telephone company defined the switchboard operators as executives so that they weren't covered by the minimum-wage law. In another case, employers would use the term "independent entrepreneur" to define the poor Blacks who gathered up sticks and brush from the woods for use in making plywood. They were paid by the load. All these silly terms and big titles were used to get around the law. I worked to get that changed.

I also tried to work on problems about which I had first-hand knowledge. For example, because of my experience overseas, I was particularly concerned about the way the workers in the American embassies and facilities were treated. Foreigners employed at the military bases and clubs were given the lowest wage possible, rather than the US minimum wage. I thought, "This is not the American way of doing things." I wanted to see that there were wage standards for overseas workers too. I thought the federal government should be an example of a good employer. I helped to create the Bill to Provide Wage Standards for Persons Engaged by Federal Contractors or Subcontractors, which Kennedy signed into law. Some of my co-workers had the text of the law bound in a little booklet and titled it, "Esther's Law."

I wanted the Labor Department to take the lead in minority hiring by bringing Black women into the Kennedy administration. When I was in New York working with the Women's Trade Union League, I got to know Dollie Lowther Robinson, a Black woman who was a laundry worker in New York. We were friends for years. I had recruited her for the Bryn Mawr Summer School; then she had served as the education director for the Laundry Workers Joint Board of the Amalgamated under Bessie Hillman. I wanted to hire her to bring into focus the concerns of Black and low-income women, the women in the sweatshops and the laundries.

Sadly, my experience with Dollie didn't work out very well. She became very close to some of the more radically activist Blacks in Washington, who instilled in her a bitterness and a claim that came out as "We want our fair share."

She had been hired to collect data on the wages and working conditions of low-income women, but she wanted to keep all her records to herself. She locked her files, even after I explained that her work was public property.

I explained that she was working at taxpayers' expense and that her data belonged to the government. She didn't appreciate that she was now a government employee; we had a program to carry out.

I finally had to let her go. It was one of the most difficult political decisions I ever had to make. We had been friends for 25 years; I loved that woman. I did everything I could to put her forward, but she made it impossible. She had such a huge chip on her shoulder that weighed her down. I don't blame her, I want to blame what was an almost evil influence over her. I think of Dollie as a victim of the times.

On November 3, 1963, I was in Seattle on my way to do a radio broadcast when the news came over the car radio that Kennedy had been shot. I had to go on the air not knowing how serious things were. In the middle of the broadcast, the announcer interrupted and said that Kennedy was dead.

Everything collapsed within me. I had had such faith in Kennedy. I had thought that he was going to build the kind of America that I wanted for myself and my children. He was our nation's future; he was our hope. America was in the midst of a social and cultural metamorphosis, and I feared that without Kennedy's leadership, our shared vision would fade.

Chapter 7

"The Most Dangerous Thing Since Genghis Khan"

In the spring of 1962 Kennedy had given the first consumer message to Congress. In the speech he stated his famous Consumer Bill of Rights: the right to safety, the right to be informed, the right to choose, and the right to be heard. This statement has become the Magna Carta for the consumer movement worldwide.

During the campaign, Kennedy had agreed to move the consumer forward. In the fall of 1960, before the election, Kennedy spoke vigorously on the subject: "The consumer is the only man in our economy without a high-powered lobbyist. I intend to be that lobbyist." Specifically, Kennedy had promised to set up a consumer advisory council and bring to the White House a representative of American consumers. I was the person he had in mind for the job.

When Lyndon Baines Johnson (LBJ) became the 36th president of the United States after Kennedy's assassination, he pledged to carry out Kennedy's consumer program. In fulfillment of Kennedy's wishes and with less than 24 hours notice, I was summoned to Texas. I was sitting in my office in the Labor Department when I got a call from Marvin Watson, LBJ's assistant. He told me to get to Andrews Air Force Base first thing the next morning to catch a plane to LBJ's ranch in Texas along with Secretary of Labor Bill Wirtz and the ambassadors to France and the United Kingdom. I knew why I was called—I had been warned—but the reality hadn't really set in. At that time, I was simply elated that LBJ was going to follow through on Kennedy's consumer program.

In Texas we were met by LBJ and Lady Bird. We rode back to the house in two golf carts; the men rode with LBJ, and I rode with Lady Bird. The Johnsons were very gracious hosts. We entered the house through the back door as though we were friends of the family. As we passed through the kitchen, LBJ asked, "Anyone want a glass of milk?" Old hats hung on a rack near the door; the place was homey and very livable.

We had lunch together, then one by one Johnson called us into his office off the dining room for a private conversation. While we were waiting, Lady Bird kept the conversation moving. Then when LBJ came in, she knew just how to let him know what was on our minds. We could chat for a few minutes, then she could give the president a 30-second summary of our concerns that was just as effective as any formal briefing. She really knew how to stand by her man.

Johnson wanted me to be the first special assistant to the president for consumer affairs. He didn't want me to give up my job at the Labor Department—I think he wanted Labor to continue to pay my salary. If I was paid by the Labor Department, it would not increase the White House staff and it would give the appearance of saving money. In retrospect, I should have known that the whole idea wasn't very important to LBJ if he wasn't willing to pay for the program or give me status as a full-time special assistant, but I accepted the job anyway.

Johnson's offer didn't exactly come as a surprise. It was really a done deal before I got there. "OK, Esther, I want you to let everyone know that I'm in their corner, and that I don't have my hands in their pockets. Now go out and have a press conference."

Now *that* I wasn't expecting. I could have fallen through the floor. I felt shaky and sweaty and unprepared. I was somewhat intimidated by the White House press corps, even though I had done a lot of public speaking and been interviewed countless times. Johnson introduced me by saying, "Now this is my gal and I want you guys out there to take good care of her." He said he wanted the voice of the consumer to be "loud, clear, uncompromising, and effective" in the highest government councils.

Of course, during the press conference I was asked, "What are you going to do?"

"I'm going to make sure that consumers understand that they have a right to be heard," I said. "I want to help consumers get a bang for their buck." Later that night my son Eric heard this quote on the radio and called me to say, "Mamma, do you know what you said? Do you know what a 'bang' for a buck is?" I didn't know what it meant. To me, I just meant that consumers should get their money's worth.

"I'm going to find out what's on people's minds," I said to the press corps. I knew I had to start where the people are. I had done that on so many other problems in the labor movement. I continued, "I intend to have conferences to hear from the people." I assumed I would have the same types of regional conferences I had had with the Women's Bureau. Ask people directly, that's the best way to find out what changes people think need to be made.

"Can people write to you?" I was asked.

I didn't even have an office, but I had to say something, so I responded, "Yes, they can write to me at the White House." I was off and running.

I got sick on my way home, and I was in bed for three days and started my new job a bit late. In just those few days that I was away, boxes of letters had collected for me at the Executive Office Building. To me it was manna from heaven. It seemed as if everyone in America had a complaint. I was receiving letters at the rate of more than 150 a day. Some of the letters were addressed to "The Consumer Lady in the White House, Washington, DC." Another said, "To The Prsdnts Asstnt on Manfctred Junk." I'm not sure how, but they made it to me.

Some letters came carefully typed on embossed stationery, others arrived scrawled on cheap notebook paper. It was clear that I was hearing from a cross section of America, and that was crucial to the success of this effort because the consumer program needed to reflect the needs of the nation.

I invited some friends from the League of Women Voters, the National Consumers League, and the American Association of

University Women to come over and help classify the letters by subject matter. People complained about problems with excessive interest rates on credit cards, product mislabeling, deceptive packaging, and misleading advertising. We learned about interest rates in excess of 200% and advertising campaigns built on illusion. In one ad, a soup company showed a bowl of soup filled with meat and vegetables. In reality the soup was filled with marbles so that the meager portions of meat and vegetables would be pushed to the top.

Reports of cases like this were the source of the consumer program; that's where the truth in lending, truth in packaging, and truth in advertising bills came from. The consumer program started from the ground up. Certainly, there was the Consumer Advisory Council that had been set up by Kennedy, but for me, the most important suggestions came directly from the people.

When I first arrived at the White House, I had to fight to build and legitimize the program. I'll never forget LBJ's assistant Jack Valenti taking me over to the Executive Office Building on my first day on the job and saying, "Here's your office. We'll get you a secretary, and that's all you'll need." I felt as if I had been duped in a major consumer fraud: the job I had just bought into had been misrepresented and mislabeled.

That's when my problems with Johnson started. I didn't want to be just a decoration; I wanted to work. My understanding with Kennedy had been that I would leave the Labor Department and work at the White House full time. I had assumed that the assignment under Johnson would be on the same terms. But I made a big mistake. I didn't establish the rules before I accepted the job.

Walter Heller, one of LBJ's economic advisors, helped me by finding a contingency fund of $10,000 to help me get the office set up. I later calculated that the yearly cost of my office—three full-time staff—was 0.0009¢ per American consumer. I didn't get any help from the Oval Office at that time; I think that I suffered because I had been a Kennedy appointee.

Walter understood how to work with Johnson. I helped Johnson draft his consumer message, but when I gave him my draft,

Johnson hated it. He asked Walter to rework it. Walter used the same material, but he broke it down into short sentences and bulleted statements, more like an executive summary than a narrative work. The words were basically the same, but they were much easier to understand. Walter taught me how to do things Johnson's way.

I ended up keeping offices at both the White House and the Labor Department. One time we had a meeting at the Labor Department and I had to scramble the three blocks between offices. Secretary of Labor Bill Wirtz introduced me at the meeting by saying that I spent two thirds of my time at the White House and two thirds of my time at the Labor Department. I did work long hours; some days from 7:30AM to 10:00PM. I couldn't have done it without my supportive staff and husband. By now, most of my kids were in high school or college. And if my schedule permitted, I made it over to watch Lars' soccer games at St. Albans.

I accepted an invitation to meet with representatives from industry shortly after I had been appointed. Boy did they go after me: "What do you know about business? What qualifications do you have to accept this position?" They found it easier to attack me personally than to deal with the issues. I was criticized as "the woman with the tight hairdo," as if my hairstyle had anything to do with the issues.

After the nastiness, Brice Harlow, one of Eisenhower's advisors, said, "Lay off her. She didn't ask for this job; she was appointed by the president of the United States." He helped get us back on track.

A lot of people in the consumer movement weren't too happy with my appointment, either. They didn't think I was qualified for the job. I was the first to admit that I didn't have the formal credentials; I was a gym teacher who didn't have any formal training in economics or law. But I understood politics, JFK had trusted me, and I knew how to consult with the experts to get things done.

Not long after I was appointed, I went to San Francisco to make a speech. I had lunch at the Fairmont Hotel with a member of the Advisory Council. She implied that I had no right to hold the job. She said that I was not qualified and that I would hurt the consumer movement. Later she became one of my strongest supporters, but her attitude fed my insecurities and undermined my confidence.

One of the first things I did was to hold the regional conferences I had talked about. We held four—in St. Louis, Salt Lake City, Detroit, and Atlanta—and they helped us establish our agenda. The *Wall Street Journal* once called me "the only woman who goes around the country hunting for bad bargains."

Our intent was to stimulate dialogue between consumers and business. At the Detroit conference, a businessman told the audience that he was sick and tired of hearing business ethics attacked. He said, "How many in the audience have ever sold a car or a house?"

A few hundred raised their hands. He said, "How many of you told the buyer *everything* he would really like to know about the true quality of the car or house he was buying?"

Only a handful raised their hands. "Ha-ha," said the businessman. "Practice what you preach."

He made his point. And at the same time many of the representatives from business got a lot out of the conferences. Most of the letters we received about the conferences were favorable. Typical of the reactions was a comment from an executive of an advertising firm who served on a food panel: "Businesses dealing in consumer goods spend millions of dollars annually in surveys designed to learn what the consumer thinks about their products and their methods of marketing them. These consumer conferences provide an opportunity to get some of these answers free."

Other businesses didn't see it that way. They considered the consumer movement a threat to business. I found that there were certain representatives from the American Retail Federation who followed me from conference to conference; I called them the "camp followers." They tape-recorded everything I said. By the third meeting I recognized them and said, "Are you guys here again? You can go and have a drink if you want because I'm going to do exactly what I did in Detroit." I tried to make light of it. They watched my every move, looking for a misstep.

A major theme of the conference was "It Pays to Complain." I told the story of when I was a child and my family lived in Arizona for a while. One day my mother sent me back to a neighbor from whom we had purchased some milk. I was to complain that the milk had been watered. "Well," said the neighbor, "I can't tell you how much water my cows drink." We got whole milk after that. It pays to speak up.

One of the common complaints we heard involved fabrics that were damaged or destroyed during cleaning. Consumers couldn't tell if a garment was safe to dry clean or if the colors were colorfast. In some situations, a dress might be laundered using one method and a collar using another. A lot of clothes were ruined because people didn't have enough information to clean them properly.

We ended up taking a pile of letters to the dry cleaners' trade association and asking what could be done to improve the situation. As it turns out, the dry cleaning industry was eager to help because cleaners had been having a difficult time figuring out how to handle all the new synthetic fabrics that were in use.

A group of representatives from the textile industry was called together. After considerable discussion, manufacturers of clothing, rugs, drapes, and other fabrics pledged not just to include a cardboard tag with each product, but to sew a tag with permanent care instructions onto every garment. I often look at the labels on clothing and wonder if people know how much work it took to get them there.

We held a "The Most For Your Money" conference involving the special concerns of low-income consumers. Grocery stores in low-income areas consistently charged about five percent to 10% more than stores in middle- and upper-income areas for the same items. We brought together a variety of stores—big and small chains, as well as mom-and-pop shops—to try to find solutions to this disparity in pricing. While there was some price gouging going on, I also learned that some small stores had to charge more because they bought in smaller quantities and because they often extended credit to customers who couldn't pay for the things they needed every week. One result was a new consumer education program in the Office of Economic Opportunity.

During my work on the conference, I handed LBJ a copy of the 1963 book by David Caplovitz, *The Poor Pay More*. I had highlighted it so that he could breeze through and not miss the most important points. He read it and supported the conference. In most cases, if I could get through to him directly, he would listen to me. He really cared about people; he was a populist, but he surrounded himself with people who didn't feel that way. When he returned the book he included a note: "Thanks, I learned a lot."

I got a lot of letters about products that break down too quickly. We divided the complaints into piles by the type of product. When a pile got to be two or three inches thick, I called a meeting of the major manufacturers and asked them how I should answer the letters. In one instance we called a meeting at the White House, and the manufacturers asked for some time to work out a solution. As a result of that meeting, the Appliance Manufacturers Association was formed.

Citizen participation was a real problem. The right to be heard was part of Kennedy's Consumer Bill of Rights, but we wanted to take things a step further and give citizen groups funding to help them have a voice in government policymaking. We wanted to have enough money to send consumers to meetings to speak up. "He who pays the piper calls the tune"—and all too often the tune is called by the deep-pocketed business community and its powerful lobbyists. It never got off the ground because there was never enough money to fund it.

One morning when Michigan Senator Philip A. Hart sat down with his eight children to a breakfast of Nabisco Shredded Wheat, he noticed the box was taller and narrower. When he compared it with an old box of cereal, he found that the net weight had dropped from 12 ounces to 10-1/4 ounces. This practice of paying for less cereal and more package was commonplace. Manufacturers found it profitable to confuse consumers.

Senator Hart responded by introducing the truth in packaging bill, which was designed to simplify the marketplace and give consumers the information they needed to make wise choices. The bill simply required a clearer statement of the contents of packages and it required that products be packaged in more standardized sizes rather than complicated fractional amounts.

At that time, products came in a dizzying array of package sizes, many of which made no sense. Take olives, for example. "Jumbo" olives were larger than the "giant," which in turn were larger than the "mammoth," which in turn were larger than the "extra large." But jumbos weren't the largest. Bigger than jumbos were "colossal." And bigger than that were "super colossal"—and the ultimate, the final word in olives, were the "special, super colossal" olives. So where did "small," "medium," and "large" fit into the picture? They were the three smallest sizes of olives.

With so many options, how could the typical shopper compare products and prices? They couldn't. I received a letter from one woman:

> I am a Vassar math honors graduate. I can't figure out the best buy between the 13 11/16-ounce jumbo size for 58¢ and the 11 3/8-ounce economy size for 47¢, especially when there's a "two-for" offer and a 4¢-off coupon (off what?) If I can't figure this out, how can the girl who didn't even finish high school?

She was right; most people didn't know how to find the best bargains. In fact, a study published in *The Journal of Applied Psychology* looked at 33 women with at least one year of college and one year of regular shopping experience. They were given 50 minutes to select the best buys in 20 product categories, even though the average shopper at the time bought 32 items in about 15 minutes. These test shoppers were right less than half the time and spent 10% more money than necessary.

I once forwarded a letter from a consumer baffled about the price of toothpaste to the manufacturer, who responded—

> Your correspondent's difficulty may be stated as follows: One large tube 1-1/16-ounce plus one family tube 5-11/16-ounce equals 6-3/4-ounce for 98¢ vs. two giant packages 2-7/8-ounces each x 2 equals

5-3/4-ounce for 98¢. It will be noted that one family size (5-11/16-ounce) has almost double the volume of two giant size (2-7/8 x 2 equals 5-12/16 ounce). In other words, one family size is only 1/16-ounce less than two giant sizes...Stating it another way: two giant 5-12/16-ounce selling regularly for 65¢ each equals $1.30, equal to 22.61¢ per ounce. One family 5-11/16-ounce selling regularly for 98¢ each equals $0.98, equal to 12.23¢ per ounce...This saving we pass on to the consumer who buys the family size rather than the giant size.

Got that?

In the letters that came pouring into my office, I repeatedly heard complaints from confused consumers—and angry shoppers. People were sick and tired of meaningless phrases like "big gallon" and "giant pint."

They were frustrated at packaging designed to deceive. I received a letter from a Texas woman who purchased her favorite face powder. She was startled to find that the price went up from $1.50 to $2.00. When she got home, she put the old and new boxes side by side and found the new box held less—two ounces instead of three ounces. She received one-third less and paid one-third more.

All too often the pictures on the packages didn't match the products inside. One woman sent me a box of frozen shrimp. Pictured on the carton were plump, luscious-looking shrimp about an inch and a half long. Inside were puny, shriveled little shrimp. I know that because she actually sent me the unused box of nasty little shrimp! Other shoppers sounded off about misrepresented banana cream pie—the box showed sliced bananas, the actual pie contained only banana flavoring; and mixed nuts—the cans show pictures of cashews and other exotic nuts, but the mixture is almost all peanuts.

Shoppers were frustrated by misleading information about serving sizes. A Rose Valley, Pennsylvania, woman complained about a can of peaches she bought for 43¢. The can said it contained six to seven servings; when she opened the can she found five peach halves, swimming in juice. "How," she asked, "do I serve the seventh person at the dinner table?"

I received letters from women complaining that they were paying $1.24 a pound for the cardboard placed under prewrapped meat. Others complained of playing hide-and-seek with meat packaging because the inferior portions were hidden from view behind opaque wrapping. A California woman asked, "Is there a possibility I could be arrested if I tear off the papers to inspect the hams before making my selection?"

Shoppers were confused by "cents off" labels. Cents off what? One person sent me two labels—one from a 10-ounce jar of instant coffee priced at $1.69 and marked 20¢ off, and a second marked $1.49 with no cents-off label. Where's the savings?

People were also frustrated at slack fill, buying huge boxes of cereal, only to open them and find them only half filled with cereal. When my kids were in the Peace Corps, I sent them packages overseas, but in preparing the boxes for shipment I would take away the excess packaging and reduce the box to the real size of the food.

I sent a letter to General Mills, suggesting that they package food in appropriate boxes for mailing overseas. I got a letter back, acknowledging that it was an interesting suggestion but that the boxes were large because the contents had a "tendency toward random directional orientation." We got such a kick out of that.

By the mid 1960s, consumers were becoming much more frustrated with their decline in purchasing power. Food prices and the consumer price index each increased about one percent a year between 1960 and 1965; they jumped by five percent in 1966. Americans were becoming less sympathetic to marketing gimmicks and deceptive packaging. It was time for Congress to act.

Hart's truth in packaging bill, formally known as the Fair Packaging and Labeling Act, passed and was signed into law in 1966 after five years of congressional inaction. The bill required packages to include labels identifying the product, the name and place of business of the manufacturer or distributor, and the net quantity of contents in terms of weight, measure, or numerical count. It was estimated to save the average American about $250 a year. When signing the bill, President Johnson called it "a weapon against high price" and said that "it reflects our strong belief that American producers can meet and want to meet the test of truth."

Misleading advertising and misleading packaging naturally went hand-in-hand. Unfortunately my campaign against false advertising was fought inside as well as outside the White House: President Johnson's advisor Jack Valenti had been head of an advertising agency and did not support my attempts to clean up the advertising industry. Valenti seemed to listen to my opponents, who charged that the plans I favored were "fuzzy, foolish, and futile" and that they would mean "devastating control." At one point I was called "the most dangerous thing since Genghis Khan."

I was accused of all kinds of things. When I was accused of putting "politics in the pantry," I responded: "Politics have been in the pantry since 1789 when the US Constitution empowered Congress to fix the standard of weights and measures. The problem is that we haven't had the consumer in the pantry."

The Michigan Chamber of Commerce called the bill
> little more than a federal grab for power to make decisions that heretofore have been made by consumers and by business—a power grab based on the fallacious concepts that the consumer is Casper Milquetoast, business is Al Capone, and government is Superman.

Others charged that the government would soon regulate that the holes in Life Savers® would have to be filled (at that point, no one had any idea that one day Life Saver® "holes" would be sold separately!). One lobbyist argued that the government would soon be telling Pepperidge Farm® that it had to make all its Goldfish® crackers swim the same direction on the package. The arguments were foolish.

Advertisers also tried to derail the bill by arguing that shoppers didn't need any extra help because they were already expert consumers. Scott Paper Company ran an ad campaign against the bill lauding the American housewife as "The Original Computer" and saying

> ... a strange change comes over a woman in a store. The soft glow in the eye is replaced by a steely financial glint; the graceful walk becomes a panther's stride among the bargains. A woman in the store is a mechanism, a prowling computer.... Jungle trained, her bargain-hunter senses razor sharp for the sound of a dropping price....

The garbage these advertisers were asking people to believe was incredible.

The American people wanted help in combating the advertising industry. Surveys conducted at the time showed that 50% of the American people believed that "most advertising today tries to deceive people rather than inform them"; 70% agreed "that the government should provide product information because producers and distributors do not give all the essential information."

One day I got a call from Valenti, who told me the president was very upset with me. "What have I done now?" I asked. He said that a big corporation had complained that the packaging bill would cost the firm millions of dollars; he said I owed them an apology. I got the brief—which was a legal size, two-inch thick document—and asked some economists to analyze it.

The company was trying to argue that it would have to change every machine to conform to the proposed laws. The whole thing was based on a false premise that extensive changes would be needed. I called Valenti and said, "I will not apologize. I am the one who is owed an apology." I never heard another word about it.

I really caught hell from both sides. Industry attacked me as a threat to the American free enterprise system; some consumer advocates charged me with being too soft. When I would get discouraged, my loving Oliver would soothe me and say, "Esther, as long as you're attacked from both sides, you can stand upright."

Things got quite nasty with the advertising industry. In 1964, only 10 months after I took office in the White House, an editorial appeared in the advertising trade publication, *Printer's Ink*, with the title: "Is She Ignorant?: Does the President Know What She Is Doing?" The article accused me of "deliberately pitting consumers against advertisers for her own purposes." They referred to me as an "articulate, ingratiating woman with the well-scrubbed exuberance of a scoutmistress leading the first hike of spring" and called my office "the most pernicious threat to advertising today."

It went on:

> She is a woman with a cause; even if her position is irrational, she presses on...she abhors persuasion, embraces the impossible idea of 'full disclosure' in advertising and would destroy advertising as it exists today. Does she comprehend what she is doing? Does President Johnson know about it?

I wanted to know exactly what Johnson thought about me, so I sent him a copy of the magazine with a note: "Am I ignorant? Do you know what I am doing?"

His response: "Definitely not, but I'm not sure just what you're doing." I didn't have the same kind of access to him that I had with Kennedy. I always had to go through Valenti to him, so I never knew whether my messages were accurately conveyed.

I am pleased to say that not everyone at *Printer's Ink* stood against me: Some admirers on the staff had a banner made that read, "*Printer's Ink* Loves Esther Peterson."

Mark F. Cooper, president and general manager of the Advertising Federation of America (AFA), sent a copy of the editorial and a memo endorsing it to all the federation members and affiliates. It seems he didn't realize that his organization had invited me to be the main speaker at their next regional meeting. I canceled the speech, saying, "The AFA believes that advertising should be completely immune from criticism. Well, the AFA is wrong." Shortly after that, another advertising group, the bigger and more prestigious American Association of Advertising Agencies, invited me to speak at their next meeting. They appreciated that all I was trying to do was to keep the advertising industry clean and honest.

In 1971 the Federal Trade Commission adopted a documentation program that shifted the burden of proof in deceptive advertising cases by requiring the advertiser to submit proof that advertising claims are truthful. Advertisers can still say,

"Palmolive® detergent softens hands," but they'll need to have the documentation to prove it.

Another major legislative battle involved Illinois Senator Paul H. Douglas' truth in lending bill. The bill was to protect borrowers from having to pay exorbitant interest rates and from being victimized in other ways by banks and loan companies and by merchants who sold goods on the installment plan.

"Truth in lending" became the catchy phrase coined to provide a simple explanation to a highly complex piece of legislation. Business interests considered Senator Douglas to be trespassing on an area rightfully reserved for private enterprise. If any abuses did exist, they said, they could best be corrected by the business groups that were most familiar with the problems.

The bill established ground rules in the credit industry. It required that people borrowing money be told the total finance charges in dollars and cents and that the true annual interest rate be revealed. This would make it easier for people to shop for loans. There are dozens of different ways to calculate interest rates, but the annual percentage rate (APR) helps to make it easier for consumers to compare rates.

At the time, there were tremendous abuses in the credit industry. Although in theory the maximum rates on credit charges were 10% for the first $500 and eight percent for the rest of the debt, because the interest could be computed in advance and added to the amount due as add-ons, the actual ceilings were close to 20% and 16% when the debt was paid within one year.

There was also institutionalized discrimination. Testimony before the Senate committee studying the truth in lending bill stated that Blacks and Puerto Ricans were systematically and automatically charged higher rates of interest than Whites.

Used car buyers were spending an *average* of 25% interest—and many paid much more. Many abuses involved no-down-payment, easy monthly payment programs to get low-income people to buy things they couldn't really afford. One witness at the hearings on the bill testified about how he bought a television set for $123.88. He was given a coupon book that called for 24 monthly payments of

$14.50—an interest rate of 229%. This man paid twice as much in interest as he paid for the television.

The truth in lending act laid the groundwork for other legislation in banking reform that has continued until today. As recently as 1991 legislation was passed requiring banks to tell savers exactly how much interest their money will earn while it is on deposit. Truth in lending and truth in saving both try to remedy a common complaint—that the true price of financial products and services is too often obscured by complexity and hidden costs.

We had a lot of trouble with the part of the bill dealing with annual interest rates. I insisted that the bill include the interest rate disclosure, but the language kept disappearing from the bill. On the day of the press conference on the bill, Johnson's chief of staff Joe Califano told me I could not attend, even though I was the special assistant to the president on consumer affairs.

I wish I could say that I had the guts to say, "Well, you can announce my resignation then," but I didn't. I just took the lumps. It may be rationalizing, but when these situations came up, I tried to keep my perspective: LBJ was so deeply involved in the Vietnam War, how could I add to his already formidable troubles? I left the White House before the bill passed, but I had done a lot of the groundwork on it.

I was never in LBJ's inner circle. There were times when I had a chance to have LBJ's ear and I didn't take advantage of it. For example, once Johnson asked me to go with him to the convention of the United Automobile Workers in New Jersey. I rode up to the convention in the back seat of the helicopter, but on the return trip I was told, "Come on, Johnson wants you to sit in the front."

I chatted with him for a few minutes about an appointment to a committee—a trivial matter—but I didn't discuss the things that were bothering me. Then he sat back and started to get sleepy. I thought to myself, "Oh, let him take a nap." I didn't feel comfortable talking to him about my problems in front of the other people on board—on the other hand, I should have taken that opportunity. I've always regretted that.

In the end, I was kicked out of the White House because I was too much of a zealot. I was pushed out; I was made so uncomfortable that I quit. I was pushed around a lot in those days. My job in the Labor Department was carved up; my work in Consumer Affairs was often undermined by Califano and Valenti. There were also petty issues, such as taking away my White House car, that were designed to bother me, to break me down little by little.

Not having direct access to the president made communication difficult. When everything I did was filtered through Valenti and Califano, I never really knew what was passed on to the president. When I met with him directly, everything went well, but when I relied on the intermediaries, we often had troubles. Johnson received written reports on my performance, because sometimes when I would meet with him he would glance at a memo then say, "Looks like you're doing all right."

I wasn't always comfortable being assertive in such circumstances. I felt as though there was a team of insiders playing against me; it was tough. We had no sisterhood then, just the old boy network, and I wasn't a part of it.

I got a great deal of support from Arthur Goldberg, but I had trouble with other men. Arthur helped me grow. As I look back, it seems that throughout my life I've had more trouble with men who didn't have professional wives. Men who appreciated their wives and valued what they did with their time outside the home were much easier to work for. Oliver never had any trouble with the work that I did; he was secure in his manliness, no matter where I worked.

Though the going wasn't always easy, I am proud of what we accomplished for consumers during the Johnson years. LBJ's legislative accomplishments were legendary; during the 89th Congress, the president asked for 113 major measures and got 97 passed. It was a period of legislative revolution, and I believe that American consumers benefited from many of those measures.

Despite the track record, the stress was more than I could take. On January 29, 1965, I sent a note to Jack Valenti: "The time has come when I need to see the president. Would you please arrange an appointment? Could it be sometime this weekend?" The end had come. I left the White House and returned full time as assistant secretary of Labor. I assumed my days in the consumer movement were over, but I was wrong.

Chapter 8

Put Up or Shut Up

I was out of a job when the Democrats were defeated in 1968, but I knew I wouldn't be jobless for long. Oliver was sick, the kids were in college, and the family needed money. I knew I would continue working and I wanted to, but I wasn't sure what I would do or what I wanted to do. So I did what seemed natural: I went back to my roots, the labor movement. I expected to fit right back into the swing of things, but a lot had changed in the years I had been away.

I returned to my union, the Amalgamated Clothing Workers of America, and continued my work as a legislative representative in Washington. My lobbying work on the minimum wage, worker safety, and other labor issues hadn't changed much, but I ran into real trouble with the union co-ops. I wanted the union stores to take the lead in acting for consumers; I wanted to put care labels in clothing and to experiment with standardization of food packaging and ingredient and nutrition labeling in the union co-ops. The union leadership didn't want any part of it. They said they didn't think the issues were important; I think they were afraid of the objections of the clothing manufacturers and afraid of the possible impact of grocery labeling on sales. They were afraid of change. I felt squelched. Here I was with my base, the labor movement, the very place I should have been able to try new things, and I was having water thrown in my face.

I think the labor movement has missed a lot of opportunities by not being more progressive, certainly in the area of consumer affairs. That kind of limited thinking keeps people down. The labor movement had a chance to show industry and other groups how to support their members in a way that is profitable for all concerned, but they wouldn't do it. From a public relations point of view, the unions could have tried a lot of cutting-edge programs and taken credit for shaping new ideas—but they didn't.

Then I got a call from Paul Forbes, special assistant to the president of Giant Food, a regional chain of 93 grocery stores in Maryland, Virginia, and the District of Columbia. I had first met Paul at President Johnson's inaugural ball. He followed up with a letter in 1965, inviting me to tour the Giant distribution center, promising "an unusual glimpse of the inner workings of the top management of a retail chain…no aspect of our operating philosophy and no area of our operations will be concealed. Your questions will be answered with complete frankness and candor."

I accepted his invitation and learned a great deal about the supermarket industry—and he learned a few things from me. For example, on the tour I picked up one of the cotton T-shirts sold under the Giant brand. I stretched it slightly and said, "I wouldn't buy that."

"Even at that low price?" Paul asked.

"No, it's no bargain." I then explained that Giant's supplier had increased production and kept costs down by cutting too many layers of fabric at one time. The bottom layers had slid slightly and were cut against the grain, something I remembered from my years working with the cutters in the clothing industry. "One time through the washer and it will be permanently out of shape," I told him.

Paul didn't want to talk about T-shirts when he called me again in early 1970; this time he wanted to talk about my coming to work for Giant. He took me to lunch at the Hay-Adams Hotel and told me that Joseph B. Danzansky, president of Giant Food, was interested in talking to me about becoming consumer advisor to Giant Food. My first reaction was that I couldn't work for industry without selling out. At that point, I wasn't even sure if the workers at Giant were unionized (they were). I felt that to work for industry would be moving over to the enemy's side. In the White House, I had spent a lot of time attacking the supermarkets, going after green stamps and packaging fraud. How could I then work for them?

Paul was very persuasive; he was always very sure of himself and confident in his ideas. I agreed to have a second lunch, this time with Danzansky. Several days later we met for lunch at Duke Ziebert's. He offered me a job as consumer advisor to the president—this time the president of Giant Food. He told me, "You've been yelling about marketing gimmicks and consumer scams for years. If you're so smart, if you know all the things we're doing wrong, it's time to put up or shut up."

He had me. I liked the idea of change because my recent experience with labor had been so sad, but I didn't want to lose my integrity by becoming a corporate puppet. I considered the offer an opportunity to have a real impact on the consumer's pocketbook; after all, at that time almost one of every four consumer dollars was spent at the grocery store. It was also a chance to make real some of the recommendations of the White House Conference on Food, Nutrition, and Health, the President's Committee on Consumer Interests, and other studies the taxpayers had already paid for while I was in office.

But I refused to become an industry flak. I knew that I would have to set strict boundaries of what I would and would not do before I could accept any offer from private industry. I had to maintain complete freedom to speak out according to my convictions, both publicly and within the company. I wanted to maintain my right to campaign for political candidates around the country and to hold offices, such as chair of the Women's National Democratic Club, a position I held at the time.

I talked it over with Oliver, and he thought I should take the job. "What do you have to lose? It's a challenge; it's time you tried a new experience," he counseled. "You can always resign if it doesn't work out."

I was concerned because I knew that I would be accused of deserting the consumer cause.

"Will you betray consumers?" Oliver asked.

"Of course not."

"Then go ahead."

Before taking the job, I consulted with my colleagues in the labor and consumer movements. I spoke to consumer advocate Ralph Nader and George Meany, president of the AFL-CIO; both urged me to take the Giant job. I knew I wanted to let my strongest supporters know where I stood, and, if possible, to get them on my side. I had learned that lesson a long time ago: Don't go out there alone. Touch base with your allies before you go out on a limb.

It was tempting. I negotiated with Giant and finally settled on a plan: I could try a number of consumer initiatives, and if, after six months, they didn't work or if the company lost money, I would have to admit I was wrong. Some people who had been my friends attacked me and charged me with selling out, but others said that I could make a bigger difference working on the inside of industry than working on the outside.

Of course, I wasn't sure that all my ideas would work, but I did trust that I knew what many shoppers wanted, because I had been shopping for my family for nearly 50 years. Some of the folks at Giant thought the programs I proposed would cost a lot of money and that consumers really wouldn't care. But I felt certain that consumers and private industry needn't be at each other's throats. What's good for consumers *can* be good for the bottom line as well.

I worked very hard to define my role clearly as the "ambassador" to the company *for* the consumer, not the ambassador of the company *to* the consumer. I was to represent every shopper, every person pushing the supermarket cart. I later tried to get this principle of loyalty and service to the consumer, not the company, as a basic statement of the Society of Consumer Affairs Professionals, but the group wouldn't adopt the platform, so I didn't join at that time. The group consisted mostly of industry people who knew their bread was buttered by the big corporations.

When I accepted the job at Giant, I didn't want to cash in. Money was not the issue. In fact, when it came to discussing salary, I said I wanted to make the same money I made in government:

$27,000. I refused to accept stock options because I thought that could be considered a conflict of interest. I couldn't have a stake in how the company did financially and still work to protect consumers. In a sense, I would have been cashing in on my reputation—and my reputation would only be of value if I didn't put a price on it.

For the most part, Giant allowed me freedom to voice my opinions, if not as a spokesperson for Giant Food then as an individual. As part of our agreement, I was supposed to be consulted on legislative issues involving consumers before Giant took a formal stand. This system usually worked well, but I once found out through someone in the office that a letter had been written from Giant to Senator Edward Kennedy that was in opposition to the position I favored for consumers. The letter had already been sent out.

I went to see Danzansky. "You have abused the understanding we had."

"What are you talking about? I assumed you had already seen the letter," he responded.

"I hadn't and I never would have allowed it to go out without a statement that I disagreed with your position." If I had known the letter was going out, I could have handled it in my own way.

Danzansky called the letter back. He got someone to telephone Senator Kennedy's office and tell them that the wrong letter had been sent and to please return it. The letter was returned, rewritten, and resent. I wouldn't allow myself to be put on record supporting—even indirectly—something that went against my beliefs.

The transition from public advocacy to private industry was not easy, either for me or for a lot of people at Giant. I went to my first meeting with all of the vice presidents and the big shots at Giant in Landover, Maryland. When I was introduced, Jac Lehrman, who owned 49% interest in the company, said, "I'm here to tell you, Mrs. Peterson, that the sooner you get out of here, the better off we'll all be."

I stood up right then. I said, "I know where the front door is. If that's the attitude around here, I'm leaving now." I was ready to quit before I got started. I'm sure part of the reason I was so feisty at Giant is that I had so often regretted not having been stronger about standing up to LBJ and his men.

Danzansky interrupted: "Esther, sit down. We're not through." He told Lehrman that I was going to stay and that the company was going to support my ideas, then evaluate my success or failure.

Danzansky carried the balance of power at Giant meetings. The Lehrman family, lead by Jac Lehrman, and the Cohen family, lead by Nehemiah Israel "Izzy" Cohen, originally owned the company jointly. But after a prolonged battle, the two families each agreed to give one percent ownership of the company to Danzansky, a successful DC lawyer who had been hired to handle labor disputes. Under the new arrangement, Danzansky's role was essentially an internal mediator. At that meeting when Lehrman tried to push me out, I remember Izzy sitting in his rocking chair giving Danzansky a nod of approval.

I knew I had the support from the top, but there were plenty of other people who assumed that I was going to waste a lot of time and money and have little, if anything, to show for it. Danzansky once was told, "If you hire that woman, not only will she be selling out, but she'll keep you from ever again selling out of anything in your stores!" When Danzansky spoke at the National Association of Food Chains' annual meeting just after I was hired, he was booed for bringing me on board. "That woman will ruin the free enterprise system," one man charged. Danzansky stood firm.

Despite the rough start, one of the first things I did at Giant was to establish a bill of rights. It was modeled on President Kennedy's Consumer Bill of Rights, but it was revolutionary for industry to stand behind the rights of consumers. Under the umbrella slogan "We're committed!" the Bill of Rights included the right to safety, the right to be informed, the right to choose, the right to be heard, the right to redress, and the right to service. Giant published a full-page ad in the local press announcing the Bill of Rights.

It was a good advertising campaign, but more important, I wanted Giant to go on record publicly supporting a statement of principles. I could use it as a bargaining tool to get certain consumer programs underway. For example, the Bill of Rights stated that consumers have the right to be informed. I went to Danzansky to discuss launching a program on open dating (to show when a product is fresh and when it is too old to sell), and I used the Bill of Rights to defend the program. When word got out, the deli manager argued, "You can't put a 'sell-by' date on a product or people will dig through the shelves to find the freshest products. It will be a mess."

"Then it's clear that you don't believe that people have the right to be informed," I said. "We'll just draw a line through that statement in the Bill of Rights." That was no idle threat; the Bill of Rights hung prominently in every store. I was sly, using the same technique I had used at the Y. First I made Giant define its principles, then I made the company live up to those principles. This time "put up or shut up" was on the other foot.

Part of my agreement when I took the job was to personally represent Giant Food in their advertising campaigns on radio, television, and in the newspapers, on the condition that I had a say in how the ads were designed and worded. Most of the ads pointed out consumer tips and weekly bargains. I soon became recognized as "The Giant Food Lady." All of the public attention made me very self-conscious when I did my family shopping. Sometimes people would follow me with their grocery carts. If I would debate between two heads of lettuce, they'd trail behind and pick the head I didn't choose when I put it back on the display. They were surprised to see me in the checkout line: "Don't you get your groceries free?" they wondered.

I found advertising a great way of talking directly to consumers, giving them information they needed to know. For example, when the price of beef went sky high in early 1972, I heard countless complaints from consumers. I knew we had to do something about it, so I called Izzy Cohen, director of operations, at 6:00AM at his home to talk about a plan. I called early in the morning because I knew he was an early riser and I could always catch him without interruption. We worked out an ad campaign calling for a beef boycott:

> You have the right to be informed
> ABOUT BEEF PRICES!
> Meat prices are high and from all predictions will remain high. Beef is near the highest level since the end of the Korean War. Why so high? IT BEGINS AT THE SOURCE: • Livestock prices were not and are not now controlled under the present economic program • Less meat is reaching the market • Prices from our suppliers have skyrocketed. Because of all these reasons, you will find higher prices on almost all fresh meats.
> We consumers can help bring prices down
> • Buy less meat • Use other forms of protein
> BUY SOMETHING ELSE

The rest of the ad suggested alternatives, including chicken, turkey, fish, eggs, cheeses, beans, and lentils. The ad mentioned that nutritional information on 85 nonbeef items was posted in all Giant stores.

It was unheard of for a grocery store to tell people not to buy beef, but that's what we did. That ad ran in a number of regional newspapers, including *The Washington Post*, *The Richmond Times-Dispatch*, and *The Maryland Gazette*, among others.

All hell broke loose. It was big news: TV crews and radio reporters wanted a comment from the grocery store that told people *not* to buy certain foods. Giant's sales increased; people shopped at our stores because they knew we were on their side. It wasn't a gimmick; it was honest. The cost of beef was too high—and there were cheaper alternatives.

After the ad appeared, the cattle industry went after me. There was even a congressional hearing during which Giant was accused of destroying the American farmer. I testified for Giant, then spent hours listening to people yell at me for telling shoppers not to buy beef. One man said, "You're taking bread from the mouths of the cattlemen's children. This is their source of income, their livelihood." I knew my position was right, but I was tired and frustrated. Throughout the hearing, Izzy Cohen sat in the back of the room listening. After the session was over, Izzy lumbered up to me (he had a bad back and found walking difficult), and he kissed the top of my head. It was his gentle way of offering thanks.

It was tough for awhile, but by the end of the year the cattle industry had gained a more balanced perspective, and the ad was selected as the best consumer ad of 1972 in a competition sponsored by the Supermarket Institute and *Family Circle* magazine.

Giant's clever advertising campaigns were good public relations, but I honestly believe they also reflected the philosophy of the company: "Good public relations is nothing more than good performance, publicly appreciated." Just do the right thing and let the consequence follow.

Of course, I also had some flops in advertising. At one point, I wanted people to know how much fat was in ground beef. Interestingly, this was 20 years before the current concern about fat in meat. We announced a 90-day test and then found that the state-of-the-art technology would not allow us to obtain accurate measurements of the proportions of fat in each category of ground beef. We had to drop the system and announce our failure. The ad boldly stated, "This test is a flop." As it turned out, it was one of the best ads we ran. We let consumers know we were willing to admit when we were wrong.

We got a lot of input from Giant shoppers. There were "Esther Peterson comment cards" available in every store. I went on radio and television and urged customers to "Speak up." I was once at the checkout counter when a woman came up to me and said, "Mrs. Peterson, will you please come and stand by me while I complain?" I took care of her complaint, and tried to explain to her that she was actually doing Giant a favor when she voiced her opinions. The company really did want to hear from her.

To process consumer complaints and to improve the stores, we set up a number of consumer advisory committees, which often had members picked from the people who wrote the most intelligent letters. I let these people suggest changes they would like to see in the stores, much like I did in my early years as consumer advisor at the White House. There were committees on nutritional labeling, ecology, toy safety, and computer-assisted checkout, among others.

The advisory committees often shaped the ideas that came directly from consumer suggestions and complaints. One woman told us that she had a housekeeper who did some cooking for the family. The housekeeper, who didn't speak or read English, served the family a pancake breakfast, topped with strawberry shampoo. The woman said the product smelled sweet and had a strawberry on the label, so she assumed you could eat it. That shopper had her breakfast ruined, but clearly the consequences could have been much more severe.

We then launched a voluntary program called "Fruit Scents and Good Sense." First, we asked manufacturers to start phasing out fruit-scented cleaning products and detergents, and we stopped packaging them under the Giant label. We displayed large posters warning consumers to be cautious of nonfood products that looked and smelled like food. We got the poison control center to tell us how many times children had to have their stomachs pumped every year because they mistakenly ate something dangerous, such as lemon dishwashing detergent or strawberry shampoo. Later, Giant was one of the groups to testify on behalf of labeling restrictions when the US Department of Agriculture (USDA) was looking into food safety, particularly the issue of nonfood products designed to look and smell like food.

Many of the letters I received at Giant echoed the complaints I had heard years before at the White House as consumer advisor. I often heard complaints about outdated products. At Giant I received a letter from a woman who bought a box of baking chocolate. When she got home, she saw on the back of the box a date indicating that the product had expired the previous year. It turns out it had been sitting on the shelf in the store for at least two years! There was no law prohibiting stores from selling outdated products, and all too often store managers weren't disciplined enough to manage their inventory properly.

The most common complaints about product dating involved spoiled dairy products. In addition to sour milk, a lot of people bought old eggs, often without knowing it. But I grew up on a farm and I knew that when the egg whites run and separate from the yolks, the eggs are past their prime. I told the dairy manager that a lot of his products weren't at their prime, and I suggested starting an experimental program with open dating, the posting of "sell before" dates that indicate when perishable products are no longer at their best.

Food processors and retailers had been dating their products for years for freshness control, but the dates were in code so that consumers couldn't understand them. When I first raised the issue, Giant rejected the idea. I was told that if consumers wanted to know about product freshness they could ask someone at the front desk to decipher the code. How many people would actually go to that trouble? I stood my ground and Giant honored its agreement to try new consumer programs. We then tested the open-dating program for six months. Consumers appreciated the program and, finally, so did Giant. It improved inventory rotation, reduced spoilage, and helped sell more Giant brand products because only Giant put dates on its store-brand goods. The consumers saved money; Giant saved money. Giant then expanded the program to include more than 400 Giant-label products, including meat and poultry.

At first, a lot of the department managers thought I was brought in as just another gimmick. They knew I had support from upper management so they had to work with me, but they didn't really think a consumer program would change anything. But the consumer program became so successful that departments inside the stores came to me and asked to be evaluated. I'll never forget when the people in the Fish Department came to me and said, "Do something to help us."

When I examined their products I saw "fresh" fish and "fancy" fish. I said, "What's a fancy fish?"

"One that has been previously frozen," came the reply.

"Then why don't we say so?"

I was told that people would not buy fish if it had been frozen. Again, I went back to the Bill of Rights. "Do we believe that consumers have the right to be informed? If not, then we'll just say, 'Except for the Fish Department, Giant Food believes that consumers have the right to be informed.'"

I was told that I was "taking the romance out of shopping." I responded, "Romance does not belong in the grocery store. There are better places for that."

Finally, we agreed to change the categories of fish. I developed an advertising campaign around a big fish in a block of ice. We offered recipes and explained to people how to select and prepare frozen fish. Again, fish sales increased because people understood what to do with the product. Consumers had the information they needed to make an informed choice.

I often traveled around the country and made speeches as a representative from Giant. One of the topics we discussed was informed choice and labeling. In Indiana I was making a speech before a grocery group and because I was a woman, many of the wives who were attending the conference were allowed to attend the speech. After I finished my remarks the chairman of the meeting said, "Mrs. Peterson, women don't want to know the contents of the food they are buying. They would never read the ingredients labels."

From the back of the room a voice interrupted, "John, we do want to know." It was his wife. Clearly these people were not listening to their customers—or to their wives.

Another project involved getting ingredient labeling on Giant brand nonprescription, over-the-counter drugs and health and beauty products. Giant bought unbranded products from independent suppliers, then put the Giant brand on the labels. The idea of listing the ingredients was new, and most suppliers feared that consumers wouldn't pay premium prices for a product, say shampoo, if they knew the most prominent ingredient was water. But Giant stuck to the program and threatened to switch suppliers if they wouldn't print the labels with an honest list of ingredients in order of predominance and without the misleading puffery, such as

"You'll look like a new woman," or "It makes you feel well." Of course, the suppliers complied. Once again, sales went up. Shoppers appreciated Giant's honesty. We take ingredient labeling for granted today, but at that time the idea of ingredient labeling was largely untested.

I got a letter from an angry shopper who read a Giant-brand product label and complained that it was mostly water. I wrote back and suggested that she find out the ingredients in the brand-name product she would otherwise use. She later wrote back and apologized because the Giant brand actually had less water than the other brand. I told that woman to be suspicious of manufacturers who advertise their creativity and expertise, then say they can't find a way to design a label telling the consumer the list of ingredients in their products.

It was even tougher to get ingredient labeling on food. I always felt that this was an even greater problem, because some people with food allergies or dietary restrictions needed to know if a product contained certain ingredients they shouldn't eat. People have a right to know what they are eating. At that time there was more information on food for cats and dogs than on food for humans.

During one discussion of food labeling one of the women on the labeling consumer advisory committee said, "Can't you just tell us what ingredients are in a product? I don't want to have to live with my fingers crossed." Her child had a problem with the eggs in certain products such as mayonnaise, and she needed to know which products contained eggs. That woman's comment made an impression on me: Consumers shouldn't have to shop with their fingers crossed.

While nutrition labeling was being debated across the country and resisted by some national manufacturers, Giant went to work on developing a plan, which became part of the basis for the labeling system that the US Food and Drug Administration (FDA) later developed. Some of the arguments against food labeling were very frustrating; industry representatives often cited the statistic that only 20% of American shoppers read labels. I considered that irrelevant. Industry had a responsibility to provide consumers with information to make intelligent decisions, whether they choose to or not. Many citizens don't vote, but that's no reason to eliminate elections. The way I see things, the low rate of label use presented a challenge to industry to design labels that are both easy to read and more useful.

We started by setting up a committee consisting of both consumers and industry. This Nutrition Labeling Advisory Committee included Dr. Jean Mayer, chair of the White House Conference on Food, Nutrition, and Health; representatives of the Home Economics Association; consumer activists; and the leading suppliers for Giant brand foods. I wanted the committee to be genuine, with representatives of real consumer groups, not the wives of the public relations people from industry. I was once asked by a business group to appear with a panel of consumer advocates; when I asked one of the "consumers" a question, she replied, "I'm sorry, my husband didn't tell me how to answer that one."

I had some trouble because I had James Turner, one of the original members of "Nader's Raiders" and an outspoken critic of the FDA and the USDA, on the committee. One industry person initially refused to sit down with "the enemy." We eventually talked both sides into working together; we developed real dialogue between groups that used to communicate only through press releases and nasty letters.

One of the committee's first projects involved percentage-of-ingredient labeling. This area soon presented a host of problems: Should the percentage of ingredients be figured before or after cooking? How should we factor in dehydrated ingredients? And how should the packing liquids be factored in?

The problems with percentage-of-ingredient labeling were causing some of the major food producers to back away from cooperating with the committee. After debating the issue, James Turner said, "I had no idea the problem was so complicated. We're not ready to deal with that issue yet." He proposed that the percentage-of-ingredient labeling issue be tabled until the nutrition labeling issue was resolved. It was a real breakthrough in communication. Neither side fully appreciated the concerns of the other until they sat down together. Again, this experience showed that once consumer activists are given some responsibility in decisionmaking, they act responsibly.

We later dealt with the technical problems of percentage-of-ingredient labeling through compromise. Instead of attempting to provide the percentages of all ingredients, the group decided to list only the amount of the major claimed ingredient. Labels would show, for example, the amount of pork in pork and beans (less than one percent) and the amount of beef in beef stew (25%).

Unfortunately, this labeling program was undermined by the USDA. The USDA said we couldn't proceed with the program because labeling beef stew as containing 25% beef would "suggest that your competitors had less than 25% beef in theirs." Eventually, the USDA allowed us to go ahead with the program, provided we put the words "government standard" on the labels.

We were able to move forward with a labeling project involving foods with a "standard of identity," a food such as ketchup or mustard that has a generally recognized meaning and a codified list of ingredients. Giant started its food labeling efforts with two such standardized products—cola and mayonnaise. The Giant experiment was supported by a group of George Washington University law students known as LABEL (Law Students Association for Buyers Education and Labeling). The group favored ingredient labeling on all standardized foods. At one point the FDA did consider requiring ingredient and nutrition labels on all 380 standardized foods, and both Giant and LABEL testified in support of the requirement. The government labeling plan failed, but Giant continued its program. The issue hasn't gone away; the government is still wrestling with food labeling and nutritional information.

Despite the frustrations and setbacks with the labeling programs, we had a lot of fun with the advertising campaigns around nutrition labeling. I did a television ad explaining Giant's new nutrition label; we had a huge can for use as a prop. It was affectionately referred to as "Esther's can." Many jokes were told about moving "Esther's can."

In addition to television spots, we also worked on other ways to get nutrition information to consumers, most notably a consumer education campaign that involved hanging nutrition information posters up in the stores above certain foods. We looked up the information from the USDA's *Handbook 8* and listed the nutritional value of fruits and vegetables and poultry and meats and breads. Each time, the sales of those nutritious products went up. I stood in the meat department and saw a woman with her kids point to the poster and say, "See, don't ever say that poor folks' food ain't good for you. Look, there's liver and greens and watermelon." I also received a letter from a 12-year-old girl who asked, "Can you please recommend some nutritious foods besides liver and kale?"

As it turned out, it was the government that made us take our nutrition signs down. I was told by a representative of the FDA, "How do you know, Mrs. Peterson, that the vitamin content of that potato is the same as the vitamin content of a potato from Maine?" It was crazy. We wanted consumers to have access to information to help them make wise decisions—and we were using the government's own data—but that wasn't good enough. The FDA wouldn't accept figures supplied by the USDA.

Another advisory committee was assigned to respond to consumer concerns about the environment. We went from department to department and considered the environmental impact of certain products. We had a lot of trouble deciding whether we should put Giant-brand milk in glass or plastic bottles. There was concern that the plastic might leech out into the milk. We did some tests and the plastic bottles proved safe, so we switched to plastic containers and told our customers what we had found. We didn't pretend to have all the answers, but we shared whatever information we had with our customers. We seriously considered their concerns, both about the environment and about their health.

Many shoppers were concerned about the presence of phosphates in laundry products because of potential water pollution problems caused by the chemicals. Giant worked with Dr. Charles Ellington, director of the Maryland State Board of Agriculture, to find a solution. Giant tested 92 products and consulted with a number of environmental experts. We learned that the experts didn't necessarily agree at that time on the ecological effects of various laundry ingredients, so Giant decided to offer several choices of ecologically acceptable products under the Giant brand—a low-phosphate detergent, a phosphate-free detergent, and a good old-fashioned laundry soap. This experiment showed us the importance of not starting a program until we've solicited expert opinions.

Giant also introduced its own line of recycled paper products, including towels, toilet paper, and napkins. I did a commercial for the Giant-brand recycled paper goods and I got an anonymous letter saying, "It's finally happened! I've seen Esther Peterson on television selling *toilet paper*." At the same time Giant launched its recycled product line, the company closed all its store incinerators and built a cardboard recycling facility that saved about 250,000 trees a year.

We knew that our customers were concerned with the safety of chemical additives, particularly FD&C Red Dye Number Two. This dye was used to color maraschino cherries, which are naturally yellow. Following the Giant policy "When in doubt, leave it out," we decided to give shoppers a choice by providing uncolored maraschino cherries under the Giant brand. Again, we found that our efforts to be sensitive to consumers' needs were stymied by the government. Once we had developed the additive-free product, officials of the FDA informed us that yellow cherries could not be labeled "maraschino" because maraschino cherries must be red! We eventually worked it out, but it shows the Catch-22 of government.

Another frustrating—but more amusing—encounter with Uncle Sam occurred when we were trying to develop nitrite-free Giant-brand hot dogs. Through proper channels and procedures we sent some of our experimental hot dogs to the USDA to be tested for bacterial growth. We didn't hear back for quite a while, so we called and found that an agency official had assumed the hot dogs were a gift and had eaten them. He liked them, and they passed the test.

The whole nitrate and nitrite issue illustrates the need to consider trade-offs in the marketplace. After developing our experimental hot dogs, we learned that the product had a shelf-life of only three days. Since consumers often keep hot dogs for a long time without freezing or eating them, we were concerned about spoilage and food poisoning. The advisory committee then recommended that the product be shelved, at least until we could come up with better technology to prevent spoilage.

This again shows the importance of working cooperatively with both industry and consumers. The consumers who participated in the development—and the ultimate rejection—of the product were no longer knocking at Giant's door asking for it. Would those consumer groups have responded the same way if Giant had simply told them, "It won't work," instead of bringing them into the decisionmaking process?

We also tried to make Giant a leader when it came to product pricing and checkout technology. Plans for Giant's unit-pricing program were under way by the time I arrived, and I appreciated the need for the program. Because the Fair Packaging and Labeling Act had not achieved standardization of packaging, we had to help provide customers with an easy-to-use yardstick for comparing prices. I knew from my days in the White House that consumers had a lot of trouble figuring out the best bargain: Which is a better deal, the 16-ounce can for 64¢ or the 5-1/2 ounce can for 23¢? The 12-ounce bottle for two for 27¢ or the quart bottle for 36¢? Fair packaging had made things better—instead of 57 different package sizes of toothpaste to choose from, the consumer had only five. But it was still difficult and time-consuming to determine the most economical purchase among the 1.75-ounce, 3.25-ounce, 5-ounce, 6.75-ounce, and 8.75-ounce sizes.

When Giant introduced its unit-pricing system it included nearly 9,000 items. Giant posted prices per unit—cost per pound, per quart, per 100 count, per square foot—to help consumers compare the real cost of one product with another. We considered posting unit-price labels on every can, then decided that shelf markers would be less expensive and equally effective. Someone actually proposed a much cheaper alternative: Supply shoppers with paper slide rules and a pamphlet on how to compute prices. But did that person have any idea how long it would take for a consumer to complete the weekly shopping and compare every price with a slide rule?

The cost of the unit-pricing program proved to be moderate: $30,000 for installation, $43,500 for remodeling after experimentation, and $10,000 for annual maintenance, or about $100 a store. From the store's point of view, unit pricing provided superb inventory control. With the shelf labels, when a store ran out of one brand of canned tomatoes, the shelf remained empty until it was restocked, making it easier for the store manager to see at a glance which shelves needed to be restocked and which products needed to be reordered. The unit-pricing system more than paid for itself by reducing price-marking errors: Before unit pricing, most stores had about 300 price-marking errors per inspection; after unit pricing, such errors were almost eliminated. A store manager who had opposed the program before it was introduced told me, "Esther, if you asked me to drop unit pricing tomorrow, I wouldn't do it. It's an invaluable management tool. It helps us run a tighter shop."

Once when I was on a Baltimore television talk show to discuss the new unit-pricing system, I brought along several products to show as examples. Just before air time, someone pointed out that one of my samples was wrong. I had with me a six-pack of Libby's grapefruit juice, listed at $3.68 a quart. The actual cost should have been 61¢, but the person who did the calculation wrongly multiplied the correct figure by six because it was a six-pack. I later found that of the 8,827 items we had in stock on the unit-pricing system at that time, there were only three errors—and I had picked one of them. I had a 2,942-to-one shot of picking an incorrect example, but I did!

Another revolutionary innovation was the computer-assisted checkout. The system, now common in supermarkets everywhere, involved the use of the Universal Product Code, the 10-digit number and bar code on every product known as the product "fingerprint." We worked with IBM to test several systems. The consumer advisory committees were very concerned about the new technology: Was it good or bad for consumers? How would shoppers know the price of the goods they were buying? How would consumers be sure the computer prices were accurate? Were there any health risks presented by the lasers that scanned the product codes?

I knew the computer was the wave of the future, but it was also very threatening to some. We needed answers to such questions, but the technology could be very good for consumers. After all, they could get a printed receipt listing all their purchases and the costs, and they could speed through the checkout lines in record time.

The computer-assisted checkout would make accuracy in unit pricing critical. I wanted every can and bottle labeled with a price tag—just as we had always done—in addition to the new unit-pricing shelf labels. I felt that in time individual price marking might not be necessary as long as people understood how to use unit pricing. We did everything we could to minimize human error. Every unit price and bar code was checked three times; I found that there were very few computer errors once the system had the kinks worked out. We tested the technology, but it didn't become widespread until years later.

One change I wanted to make at Giant but was never able to achieve involved the way products are arranged on supermarket shelves. The big suppliers of brand-name products insisted that the displays be to their advantage, with their products at eye level. I wanted to rearrange the shelves for consumer convenience, not brand loyalty. I didn't think it was fair to show preference for one manufacturer over another. But this was considered a marketing issue, and my efforts went unheeded. This was my first hint at how powerful the big corporations actually were at shaping the marketplace.

I consider my years at Giant to be among the most productive and useful of my life. Not only was I able to be part of some important changes in the food industry, but my Giant years also proved that constructive relationships can be built between consumers and business. At Giant, I always tried to find common ground between consumers and business and to develop programs that were mutually beneficial. Though it's difficult to establish a direct correlation between the introduction of the consumer programs and the bottom line, during Giant's 1972 fiscal year, the first full year the programs were in place, the company set records in both sales and earnings. One man told me, "I bought Giant stock because of you."

Credit goes to Danzansky. He had the courage to back me up and to try new ideas. He also had a strong sense of community values. He knew that the poor paid more at the mom-and-pop shops in the inner city than other people paid in the suburbs. He had opened a big market on 14th Street in DC and kept the prices low, the same as in the suburbs. He trained people in the neighborhood and gave them jobs. That sometimes led to problems when friends would come into the store and ask the manager and employees for free food. One time the manager of the 14th Street store came to Danzansky and offered to quit. He said he couldn't take the pressure anymore of his friends stealing and then asking, "Are you one of us or aren't you?" Danzansky transferred the manager to another store so that he could keep his job. Despite the problems, Danzansky was right: That store belonged to the community. In fact, during the riots in the 1960s that was one of the few stores in the area that wasn't damaged. The community felt it belonged to them.

Over the years, a lot of people in industry, including Robert Aders of the Food Marketing Institute, changed their opinions about me. When I was introduced to a business group in my early years at Giant, I was greeted as "The woman who sends shivers up and down the spines of virtually all business people." Later, I was honored by the grocery industry itself when the Food Marketing Institute, the supermarket trade association, established the Esther Peterson Consumer Service Award. It is named after me because, they say, I did so much to revolutionize the food industry. Each year it is given to a person whose professional life has served the consumer. I feel honored, not because the award bears my name, but because it comes from an industry that considered me an opponent for so many years. To be recognized by your former enemies is indeed an honor.

But despite my success at Giant—which exceeded all my expectations of seven years before—I left private industry in 1977 when President Jimmy Carter invited me back to the White House as special assistant to the president for consumer affairs. I would have loved to have stayed on at Giant—there was a lot more work to do. I wanted to tackle some of the problems Giant had as a consumer, such as fading ink, defective frozen food cases, and frozen foods that were spoiled from being allowed to thaw and refreeze. In the food industry there is always change; the job of consumer advisor to a grocery store chain could easily be a lifetime profession. Though I was proud of the work I did for the president of Giant Food, it's hard to resist a call from the president of the United States.

At my farewell party from Giant, Paul Forbes presented me with a touching gift: a can of Giant Food Home Style "Essence of Esther." The list of ingredients included enormous heart, a trick knee, and no artificial anything. The preparation instruction read: "Combine contents with equal parts of politics, business sense, street savvy, and activism. Avoid boiling. Garnish with finely chopped chambers of commerce. Serve generously for the consumers of America."

The bottom of the can read: "NET WAIT: At least four more years."

Chapter 9

Back to the White House

When I worked at the White House I always entered the Oval Office through the side door, but when I went to meet President Jimmy Carter for the first time, I went in through the front door, as a formal visitor.

When the president introduced himself, he put his arm around me and kissed me. I knew he did that sort of thing, but it still made me feel good; I felt that he really wanted me to be a part of his team. I liked him immediately; I knew we could work well together. The chemistry was good.

I was impressed that President Carter had spoken out strongly for consumer issues during the campaign. He stressed his support for a strong government agency to represent consumers, and in his presentation to the Democratic Party Platform Committee at the nominating convention he called for "major reforms to protect the consumers of this country."

I hadn't worked with Carter before, but it was clear that we had both heard a lot about each other. It seemed that he had heard that I was a good lobbyist and he had a consumer bill he wanted me to get through Congress.

In the middle of the meeting, in walked Fritz Mondale. I knew him from my days on Capitol Hill, and I wasn't sure if I was supposed to report to Mondale or to the president. "To whom do I report? Who will be my boss?" I asked the president. Carter responded, "You better report to me. Mondale will be too hard to reach."

I took the job, and my title once again was Special Assistant to the President for Consumer Affairs. The big assignment was to lobby for the Consumer Agency Bill. Carter wanted to create an independent office within the federal government that would handle consumer issues and advocate the consumer point of view in hearings before federal agencies and courts. He wanted a body to plead the consumer's case with the federal government.

The agency bill called for the consolidation of 26 existing consumer programs scattered throughout the federal bureaucracy into a single, independent agency with the authority to intervene in policy matters affecting consumers. The bill would save taxpayer dollars by streamlining government and avoiding duplication of activities.

The bill was vigorously opposed by businessmen, who used many of the same tired arguments used when we were getting the consumer movement off the ground years before. Business called a high-level consumer body "a form of harassment which keeps [business] from operating freely and independently." The bill was also called a "Trojan Horse Threat to American Business."

I was in the job as special assistant to the president for only one day before the hearings on the bill began, so I spent my entire first day becoming familiar with the president's position. I met with every member of the House Government Operations Committee; the attitudes of the legislators clearly showed that business had been there first. The impression among many people was that the bill would simply create another federal agency, another layer of bureaucracy that would cause regulatory delays.

Campaign contributions had a lot to do with it. One member actually told me, "The Chamber of Commerce will hang me if I vote for this bill." Another said, "I'll vote for it—if you can come up with the $100,000 in contributions that it will cost me if I do."

The agency bill had grassroots support, as was indicated by Ralph Nader's "Nickel Brigade"—the nickel representing the cost of the agency to each taxpayer. Nader and a number of other public interest organizations selected 78 target districts, then gathered signatures and nickels to be mailed to the appropriate legislators. In two months, 400,000 nickels flooded Capitol Hill.

Despite Ralph's innovative campaign, I had a lot of trouble with him. Legislators who didn't support the bill caught hell from Ralph. Ralph was good at getting people to take a stand, but he didn't appreciate that I was working behind the scenes to build support for the bill. Ralph did not appreciate some of the subtleties of lobbying. It's not an all-or-nothing game. It seemed to me that he couldn't always tell who needed honey and who needed vinegar.

I got quite a few calls from people saying, "Esther, I'd like to help you, but Ralph is out saying that I should be defeated when I run for re-election."

I had to go to Ralph and ask him to stay away from certain districts; we had the same goals, but I had my own way of getting things done. He favored confrontation; I favored persuasion. I wanted to go in through the back door sometimes, but he always wanted to fight very publicly. It was really just a different way of working; Ralph's methods can be very effective, but we just happened to clash.

My greater problem was Frank Moore, Carter's assistant for congressional affairs. He had handled Carter's legislation in Georgia, which, in my opinion, didn't qualify him to become the president's chief legislative representative in Washington. Moore just didn't know his way around Capitol Hill, and he certainly didn't understand vote counting.

Just before the vote on the Consumer Agency Bill, I saw Frank sitting on the davenport in Tip O'Neill's office. He was talking about how close the vote was going to be. I said to him, "Frank, those extra votes are not going to come from that davenport. For hell's sake, get out there and do some lobbying." I still don't know if he was lazy or if he genuinely did not understand Washington politics. I sometimes wondered if he really was in favor of the bill. I know I sound harsh, but I really wanted that bill.

The problems came to a head on the day the Consumer Agency Bill was to be voted on. The vote was going to be very close; I had been counting noses. I figured that we might lose by two or three votes, but even if we did we would show a lot of support, so we could pick up the bill again. I was thinking of the long run; I know that things don't happen overnight—especially on Capitol Hill.

The vote had been scheduled for November 2, and I was working hard on contacting as many uncommitted members as I could. On the morning of November 1, I was on the House side and I learned that Frank Moore was in the speaker's office. I rushed over and Moore asked me to sit down. He said he didn't think the votes were there yet. I explained that my vote count was a bit more optimistic than his, but there certainly was more work to be done before the end of the day.

I went to a brief lunch on the Senate side, and I was stopped by several people who said I was wanted in the speaker's room. Moore had decided to pull the bill from the calendar. Moore made this decision without consulting me, even though I was supposed to be in charge.

I was irate. I called Stu Eizenstat, Carter's domestic advisor, and blew my top. I wanted to get away from Washington, so I took the next plane to visit my family in Utah. I had to escape; I couldn't stand it anymore. I was also afraid the press was going to ask me questions, and I would have to answer honestly. When I got to the airport in Salt Lake City, I was greeted by an airport official who asked me to go to his office: "The president of the United States is calling you."

When I picked up the phone, I was still mad. I told him, "Mr. President, you can have my resignation right now, if you want it. Frank Moore is not serving my interest, your interest, or the consumers' interest. This is the worst operation I have been part of in all my years in Washington." I just let it all out. I felt a great relief to get it all off my chest, then I thought to myself, "Here's the end, Esther, hurrah."

Instead of accepting my resignation, Carter said, "Esther, calm down. Don't be rash. You don't have to decide anything until you get back."

My warmth for him returned. One of his strengths was his ability to not let egos get in the way of getting work done. He accepted my anger and never held it against me. There was still a lot of work to be done, and I agreed to stay on.

When I got back from Utah, I talked things over with Carter and it was decided that the bill would be an administration bill for the next year. Carter asked me to stay on to work on it. I agreed.

I felt that when the new Congress convened and this first administration bill was to come up, the vote would be key to setting up momentum either for—or against—Carter's legislative program. The bill had a lot of support, but I felt that if the opposition could kill this bill, they could kill all of Carter's bills.

I went to a cabinet meeting and expected Carter to call on me to comment on the bill; he didn't. At the end of the meeting I went up to him and said, "Mr. President, this is precedent setting. If we lose this bill, we'll lose them all."

The only one to support me was Bob Strauss, who pointed out, "You know, Esther's right on that." Carter didn't understand and Frank Moore didn't understand. They didn't use the telephone, they didn't work the votes. Johnson would have three telephone lines at work when he was making personal calls about a bill; I don't think Carter really knew how to make the system work for him. Carter never used the power he had. Goodness does not necessarily prevail; it has to be assisted, and I'm not sure that Carter understood that.

As the bill was doomed, Carter decided to issue an executive order establishing a Consumer Affairs Council, consisting of high-level representatives of major federal agencies. It also established a voice for consumers within the government by designating a government official purely responsible for defending the consumers' interest in policy development and rulemaking. This person was to have the ear of the secretary of the agency, so that consumer issues would not be lost in the bureaucratic maze. The goal was to get the government "to think as a consumer would think." I think Johnson was on the right track when he said, "Let's make the good practices of the marketplace the common practices." Businesses had always had lobbyists on hand to explain their side of an issue during the regulatory process, but before Carter signed this executive order, consumers were rarely represented.

Carter also went a long way toward defending consumer interests by appointing regulators who believed in the consumer. Carter's team—including Mike Pertschuk as chairman of the Federal Trade Commission, Joan Claybrook as administrator of the National Highway Traffic Safety Administration, Carol Foreman as assistant secretary of agriculture for Food and Consumer Service, and Eula Bingham at the Occupational Safety and Health Administration—these people were all believers. They worked to get the regulations on the books, and they strongly supported their enforcement. One of the phrases we used was "a law not enforced is a no-law."

In the Johnson White House, consumer issues were dealt with separately, but in the Carter administration we worked together as a team. We took into consideration the impact of policy on consumers and citizens, not special interests. In the Carter White House we consulted with one another; I was always able to add what I felt was important to various programs put forward, even if they were not strictly consumer initiatives. As a result of our cooperation, the Carter administration did a lot to move consumers forward.

Within the Office of Consumer Affairs, we did a lot of work to fight inflation. Inflation was going crazy, and we wanted to create a program that would involve voluntary cooperation. The Office of Consumer Affairs wrote to the 50 largest food chains and the 50 largest drug store chains and asked that they voluntarily freeze the prices on commonly used store-brand products. More than a dozen chains, 7,500 stores, responded by setting ceilings on prices for between one and six months. Stores couldn't freeze the prices of name-brand products, but they could control the prices on their own products.

This project was a direct outgrowth of my work at Giant; I already knew the people, and I knew we could work together. I got Giant to be one of the first to put the price ceiling on Giant brand products. I knew there had to be an economic incentive to all this and there was: People bought more of the store-brand products when the prices were lower, and the public appreciated the effort of the supermarkets to hold down inflation.

I remember sitting around a table in the "Fish" room (now the Roosevelt Room) at the White House during a meeting of the top executives of the supermarket chains. I had talked most of them into participating in the program, but Robert Aders from Kroger sat in a chair in the corner and did not enter into the discussion. He resisted the program at first, but eventually he accepted it and became one of my best friends in the supermarket industry.

As part of my department's work to fight inflation, we wrote a 411-page book titled *People Power: What Communities Are Doing to Counter Inflation*, which included 338 first-hand examples of things people were doing to help control their finances. We sent it free to anyone who wrote to the White House for a copy. We mentioned local groups that started food co-ops, built housing for the elderly, installed windmills in community gardens, and lobbied against utility rate increases. Our press people collected clippings of consumer activities all over the country, then I visited a lot of cities and wrote up the activities to inspire others. We officially released the book at the Low-income Consumer Self-Help Conference. We wanted everyone to know that his or her voice counts.

The project got mixed reviews. Lloyd Cutler, legal counsel to President Carter, gave me a lot of grief because he thought the project wasn't "White House caliber." On the other hand, Ralph Nader in his syndicated newspaper column called it "400 free pages of good stuff." *The New Republic* criticized the entire premise: "Local communities can do about as much to stop inflation as they can to free the hostages in Iran...Inflation is a national problem that can be solved only by national government policy." They just didn't get it: The point wasn't to solve the nation's economic woes, it was to help the Little Guy make ends meet during difficult times.

The Carter administration took a lot of steps to protect the Little Guy. Carter signed a bill allowing savings and loan associations and commercial banks to issue certificates of deposit and to increase the rate of interest they pay to small savers. Before then, people who invested small amounts of money earned considerably less than those able to save larger sums.

We got energy-efficiency labels on products; we pushed for a program for simplified English in government documents; we established consumer rights to itemized prices from funeral homes. When the funeral industry argued that people couldn't deal with price information at such a difficult time, I responded, "If there's one time when consumers are vulnerable, it's when they've lost a loved one."

We established consumer rights regarding overbooked airline flights; we started a cooperative bank so that public-interest groups could obtain low-interest loans; we increased competition in the trucking industry; and we published a consumer resource handbook to help people figure out which office or agency they need to call to file a complaint or get information; it's still one of the most popular government publications for consumers.

Consumer Affairs worked with Joan Claybrook at the Department of Transportation on the fuel economy rating of cars. We also rated different makes and models of cars for their safety and expense in terms of both maintenance and repair. The Office of Consumer Affairs opposed the lowering of the automobile bumper standard from five miles per hour to 2.5 miles per hour—a change that would have cost consumers an estimated $400 million in increased repair bills. I went to Detroit with Joan and drove around in a test car when meeting with automakers to discuss the programs.

We published a "Consumer Action Update" to help consumers find out what proceedings were going on in federal agencies. The update included a list of the significant issues and the names and phone numbers of the government officials who could be contacted for more information. In addition, the *Federal Register* initiated a special index that highlighted proceedings and notices of special interest to consumers. We tried to bring government to the people. Carter was in total support of getting the consumer involved.

Of course, it wasn't always easy, and we didn't always get along. One person I had difficulty with was Lloyd Cutler, legal counsel to the president. The most telling example of our conflict came up when I was invited to Union Station to speak at a big consumer rally sponsored by Ralph Nader and Mark Green. I had accepted the invitation, but Cutler didn't want me to go. He asked to review my comments, and he gave me some prefacing remarks to read before I made my speech:

> My remarks today are my personal views, not the views of the White House. While every group in our society is open to legitimate and constructive criticism, I do not believe in attacks on business or big business as such. Business and big business are a creative and vital force in our free American society.... I disassociate myself from putting big business on trial and from the flysheet distributed for this meeting featuring my name and title with such pejorative catch phrases as "Tour of the Corporate Hall of Shame" and "Learn How To Fight Crime in the Suites."

I was appalled that Cutler wanted to put words in my mouth. Someone on my staff had prepared a draft of a speech, and it wasn't appropriate and I wasn't planning to use it. In most cases, I spoke extemporaneously. In the end, I made the speech— without his additions— and nothing more was said of the matter. Cutler was influenced by the wishes of industry and it showed.

In 1979 and 1980 one of the biggest battles facing the Carter administration involved an attempt to undermine the consumer protection activities of the Federal Trade Commission (FTC). Under the vigorous leadership of Mike Pertschuk, the FTC had become dangerously effective in the eyes of business. A Chamber of Commerce representative even joked about "membership in the FTC victims' alumni association." To counter the attacks from the Chamber of Commerce, consumer and labor groups got together and formed the Consumer/Labor Coalition to Save the FTC.

This was a period of corporate backlash, an all-out assault on "big government." The FTC was called the "Tyrannosaurs rex" of the regulatory agencies, and legislation was introduced to curb its powers. As a result, legislation that had been coyly labeled the "FTC Improvements Act" had passed both the House and the Senate. It would have removed the FTC's jurisdiction in many areas of the economy. Carter threatened to veto any bill that crippled the FTC, but the bill was moving forward.

It was a tense time. Carter ordered us to drum up support for his position. He really saved the FTC. At a meeting with Mike Pertschuk and several staff people from the Senate and the House, Carter analyzed the bills on the FTC section by section. He knew exactly where he would draw the line—what could stay in and what would have to go for him to sign the bill. It was a difficult meeting, and I didn't learn until much later that while Carter was presiding over that meeting about the FTC, he knew that his ill-fated mission to rescue the Tehran hostages was under way. I don't know how he could conduct a meeting with this other issue pressing so heavily on his mind, but he did. I think that shows the strength of that man. When you talk about being presidential, he was.

One of the toughest—and one of the most important—issues we wrestled with involved Executive Order 12160. It started when I was notified about the problems with TRIS—also known as (2,3-dibromopropyl) phosphate—a flame retardant on children's sleepwear that had recently been shown to cause cancer. In April 1977 the TRIS-treated sleepwear was banned for sale in the United States, but US companies continued to dump 2.4 million pieces of TRIS-treated sleepwear in overseas markets for more than a year.

"This is a consumer issue, Esther," Carter said, appointing me and Robert Harris of the Council of Environmental Quality as cochairs of a 24-agency panel to deal with the problem. Our group, the Interagency Working Group on a Hazardous Substances Export Policy, worked on it for two and a half years, discussing the issue with chemical companies, export industries, and all the cabinet officers who dealt with the export of American products.

Our TRIS task force wrote an executive order mandating that the US publish a list of products banned in this country. The list would then be sent to all our embassies and distributed to countries importing US goods. The executive order did not forbid countries from accepting goods banned in the US, it merely stated that countries would have to give prior informed consent. Some products—especially medicines—that are banned in the US might be needed overseas. These countries could obtain what they needed, provided they accepted the risk. It all came back to Kennedy's Consumer Bill of Rights—the right to be informed.

I discussed the issue with Lloyd Cutler. "It's too late," he said. "An executive order like that would be too damaging to the president politically."

"That's a decision for the president to make," I replied. We had worked far too hard to let Lloyd Cutler stand in the way.

A lot of presidential advisers thought the executive order was political suicide. We brought it to the president anyway, and he signed with less than a week remaining in office because he considered it the right thing to do.

After the 1980 election, it seemed the entire country was gearing up for a Ronald Reagan presidency. I'll never forget attending a cocktail party when a lobbyist from a pharmaceutical company who was a little bit drunk said to me, "You're just batting your head against the wall. We'll get rid of Carter and we'll get rid of controls on exports."

As predicted, a mere 34 days after taking office, President Reagan withdrew the executive order, leaving other countries in the dark about the possible hazards presented by certain American goods. Reagan said more study on the issue was needed, and he appointed Secretary of State Alexander Haig and Secretary of Commerce Malcomb Baldridge to look into it. In my experience, when a president orders more study, it usually means he doesn't want to face the consequences of making a real decision.

At home, the Carter years were trying years. For a number of years, Oliver's cancers had been watched carefully by doctors at the National Institutes of Health. In 1979 I went with Oliver to a doctor's appointment where they put dye in his body and put him under a machine that showed where the cancer was. He lit up like a diamond. I could see the cancer. It became even more real.

We asked the doctors how much longer he had to live. They said they weren't sure, but if there was something important for him to do, now was the time to do it.

Oliver wanted to see our daughter, Karen, again. She and her husband and three children were in Lesotho working on an Association for International Development project; her husband was an economic geographer. We flew to South Africa, then went into Lesotho. We were having a great visit, but then when we were having a dinner party, Oliver excused himself and went to lie down. I went in to check on him and he was burning up; I think his fever reached 104 degrees.

We drove to South Africa to find a decent hospital; the medical facilities in Lesotho were embarrassingly bad. Karen and I and the children took a hotel room by the hospital. When his condition stabilized, we wanted to get him home. We had to have a row of seats across the airplane so that Oliver could lie down during the flight. Lars met us at the airport with the station wagon fixed up with a bed in the back, but we didn't need it.

As soon as Oliver's condition improved, we went home to Vermont. For a while he was stronger, but then he started having more difficulty. He fell out of bed one night and broke a hip. It seems the cancer had spread to his bones as well. Cancer—God damn that disease.

On May 10, 1979, my precious Oliver died. We had a simple service at the Townshend Church in Vermont, and that night the family had supper together around a bonfire up on the hill behind the farm. Later, when all the visitors had gone home or to bed, the kids and I—with the strength of being together—spread Oliver's ashes by moonlight on the hill he loved so dearly.

Chapter 10

Will "Made in America" Become a Warning Label?

I wondered to myself, "What's next?" After leaving the White House I became something of a professional consumer advocate on television and radio. But the work was getting stale; I needed something new. I felt that all I was doing was recycling what I had done before.

Then I got a call from Rhoda Karpatkin, executive director of Consumers Union and the president of the International Organization of Consumers Unions (IOCU). I had always been somewhat afraid of her; she is a brilliant, well-trained lawyer and consumer advocate. I felt she had so many skills that I didn't have. I was in awe of her abilities; I wished I could be more like her. She wanted to know if I would be interested in volunteering to represent IOCU at the United Nations (UN).

Of course I was interested. It was a whole new field to try, and I could see from my experience with the TRIS episode in the Carter administration that consumer issues were becoming global concerns. And, in a way, it was a natural fit. I had spent a number of years living abroad, and I had traveled extensively—from Vik, Norway, to Timbuktu, Mali. I appreciated the contrasts in consumer protection programs between developed and developing countries.

IOCU had been represented at the UN by Dorothy Wilner, the wife of a very successful businessman. She had been able to get IOCU Category One status, the top consultative status given to just a few nongovernmental organizations. This was no small feat; Dorothy worked very hard to put IOCU forward. But she had some difficulties with interpersonal relations both at IOCU and at the UN. I was not aware of these problems when Rhoda called me. I wonder if I would have accepted the job if I had known the depth of the problems with Dorothy; the last thing I wanted to do was walk into the middle of a hornet's nest of personal conflict. She was so sure she was right. It was difficult to have conversations with her that were open to change.

I accepted Rhoda's offer. It was a volunteer job, but I knew it was an important one. I honestly didn't understand global economics; in college I only got as far as Economics 1—and we didn't make it beyond the economy of the US! But I did feel that I could learn, and I hoped that I could make a bit of a difference to some people, especially those in less developed countries.

On a personal level, I also wanted to take the job to show Ronald Reagan that he did not have the final word. Reagan had canceled President Carter's executive order creating the list of banned products in the US. Like Carter, IOCU believed that a document should be published listing products banned from sale in the country of manufacture, so that countries importing these goods could make informed decisions about whether to accept them. IOCU was already at work on the publication of a similar list through the UN, and I was asked to help.

Rhoda told me that the representative from Venezuela was livid that Reagan had canceled the list. He had told her how much he needed the list and asked her to see if she could get "that woman from the White House" to help lobby for IOCU to get it through the UN. That cinched it for me.

The idea of publishing a list of banned products wasn't new to the UN. In fact, the General Assembly first took up the issue in 1979 when it passed a resolution urging exporting countries to notify importing governments of the risks of hazardous products. During the next several years the idea of a list of banned products was discussed in the Economic and Social Council. In 1982 the UN passed a resolution stating that products banned in one country should be sold abroad only when the importing country requests the product or when consumption is officially permitted there.

More important, the 1982 resolution also directed the UN secretary general to prepare, publish, and regularly update a list of products that have been banned by any country. This list would encourage informed consent, and it would discourage deceptive and dangerous practices in the international marketplace. When the final vote was taken, the resolution was favored by every nation but one—the United States of America.

How could the US possibly object to the list? The rationale offered by US delegate Dennis C. Goodman was that the information could be misleading and dangerously prejudicial. Instead, the US favored an index of potentially troublesome substances and products. The index would contain the name of the regulated products, the name of the country imposing the regulation, and the full address for more information. I felt this cumbersome process would make it difficult—if not impossible—for many countries to investigate all the products it considered for import.

The US also objected to the cost of the list: $1 million for publication in six languages. If the list must be published, the US favored the release of only a single volume, written, of course, in English. The Reagan administration argued that the publication was wasteful because the information was generally available elsewhere, although not in one place. I asked some of the people in the US trade office how I might go about tracking down the risks of a particular substance, and they were stumped. Sure it could be done, but few countries would have the resources and time to do the research necessary—so much for Kennedy's consumer right to be informed.

One of the most effective lines I heard during the debate about the Consolidated List originated with Anwar Fazal, then president of IOCU. In an impassioned speech during a radio interview, he said, "Will 'Made in America' become a warning label, instead of a sign of quality?" That comment sent a shiver down my spine; I've used it countless times when describing the importance of the list.

Representatives from many countries, especially those in the Third World, were dismayed at the US position. Ironically, the debate over the final acceptance of the Consolidated List took place at the same time reports came in describing the disaster in Bhopal, India, in which 40 tons of poison gas escaped from a plant owned by an American company, the Union Carbide Corporation. More than 3,000 people died in the accident. The chemical involved in the Bhopal disaster wasn't on the list of banned products, but the tragedy does show the lack of information many countries are given about the potential hazards in their midst.

Throughout the process, the US was uncooperative and unresponsive to UN requests for information. When the UN was preparing an initial draft of the list, the US simply refused to comply with the request to provide information on restricted products. The US argued that there were technical problems associated with the task, particularly difficulties in identifying all the products that might fall under the "banned," "severely restricted," or "not approved" categories. In the end, we filed various requests under the Freedom of Information Act and conducted our own research in the *Federal Register* to obtain the information. The US government dragged its feet all it could, but eventually democracy prevailed. We got the information, though we had to track it down ourselves from a number of sources.

The program was desperately needed. The Third World had become the international dumping ground for defective medical devices, lethal drugs, contaminated foods, dangerous pesticides, and other hazardous products banned from US markets. Products that our government deemed unsafe for US citizens were shipped abroad for use by unsuspecting people in other countries. For example—

- Of the pesticides exported in 1976, 29% (161 million pounds) were not registered for use in the US, and 20% of those (31 million pounds) had been banned by the Environmental Protection Agency because they posed unreasonable hazards to human life, wildlife, or the environment.
- The pesticide DBCP, a soil fungicide, was banned from the US market in 1979 (except for use on Hawaiian

pineapples) because it proved carcinogenic and mutagenic in animal tests and caused sterility in workers in manufacturing plants. Four years later, DBCP was still produced for sale in foreign countries.

• The analgesic dipyrone was removed from the US market by the Food and Drug Administration in 1977 because it had been shown to cause a fatal blood disorder and had been implicated in several deaths. Six years later, US companies continued to sell the drug in Latin American countries for use against minor ailments, with no warning concerning its dangerous side effects.

While the situation is improved, banned products are still sent overseas. In 1993 the US Office of Technology Assessment examined product labeling by US-based multinational pharmaceutical companies for the drugs they sell in developing countries. Of the 241 drugs sampled, fully two-thirds failed to provide the labeling information a physician needs to use the drugs safely and effectively.

Another very real problem involved misleading advertising and promotion. I saw a calendar by DuPont in Southeast Asia that showed photographs of scantily clad women spraying pesticides; they should have been wearing protective clothing. Not only were dangerous products sold abroad, but the instructions and labels were written in languages many foreign workers could not understand. My experience in the labor movement made me particularly sensitive to these issues; it was the workers in the fields who ultimately suffered because they were the ones exposed to the dangerous chemicals. It both saddened and angered me to realize how cheap life was to so many huge corporations.

The list—formally titled the *United Nations Consolidated List of Products Whose Manufacture and/or Sale Has Been Banned, Withdrawn, Severely Restricted or Not Approved by Governments*—is prepared by the UN secretariat. At the end of 1983 the UN completed the first draft of the Consolidated List, a document that ran more than 500 pages. It wasn't the official list because it had not yet been formally approved by the General Assembly. It covered more than 400 products, including pharmaceuticals, pesticides, industrial chemicals, narcotics, and consumer products. Of course, the volume wasn't comprehensive—just because a product was not on the list did not mean it was safe. And the reverse was also true: Just because a product was on the list did not necessarily mean it would not be appropriate for use under certain circumstances.

The Consolidated List has had a significant impact on a number of countries. For example, the Citizens' Alliance for Consumer Protection of Korea has used the list to monitor how many banned pharmaceutical products were sold in their country. The results: in 1986, 29 hazardous ingredients were manufactured into 232 drugs. The group asked the Ministry of Health and Social Affairs to take action, and the government banned 24 drugs and restricted 27 others in 1988.

In Ecuador an environmental organization used the list to convince the minister of agriculture to ban or restrict the use of all organochlorine pesticides, the class of compounds made famous by Rachel Carson's book *Silent Spring*. These chemicals, including such pesticides as DDT, were banned or restricted in most developed countries in the 1960s, but they are still used in other parts of the world.

Today the list is uniformly accepted. In recent years, when the issue of updating the list has come before the UN, there has been no opposition to it—not even from the US.

At the same time that the Consolidated List was being negotiated, I was also working on the United Nations Guidelines for Consumer Protection, a set of standards to help developing countries establish consumer protection programs modeled after those in the US. The guidelines include broad statements on matters such as product safety, consumer redress, and consumer education, as well as guidelines on specific areas, such as food, water, and pharmaceuticals. It would be up to each country to decide how to use the guidelines.

What we really wanted was for consumers in other countries to have some of the same consumer protections we enjoy in the US.

As part of our effort, we got a Georgetown University law group to take our US laws and to compare them with the consumer guidelines that had been drafted by IOCU. I used this document to show how the guidelines were basically an extension of the laws already in place in the US. After all, if consumer protection is good for the US, why isn't it good for other countries too?

What it all comes down to is that, ready or not, we're a global economy now. When I was lobbying I often used the phrase, "We need to avoid creating an international Love Canal." Corporate misdeeds can boomerang on us; the toxins the US might dump overseas may someday wash back up on our shores. Even if we don't have any concern for the other countries, we should at least have a selfish concern for our own well-being.

The business community fought every step of the way. During one particularly tense negotiation, I went to the room where a discussion was being held and I was asked to leave. I believe the person asking me to leave was Alan Keyes, the representative from the US. I firmly told the person ejecting me that I had Category One clearance, which carries with it the authority to attend certain sessions. I then looked across the room and saw the representative from the International Chamber of Commerce, another Category One group. I demanded that if I had to go, he did too. "If he doesn't come out, I'm going back in," I argued.

A few minutes later the Chamber of Commerce representative joined me in the hallway. We were both angry; we had a right to attend that meeting. After the meeting we confronted the chair of the meeting and established our right to attend later meetings; we had no problem getting into subsequent sessions.

Some lobbyists from multinational corporations were able to convince the government to propose a compromise that would have gutted the guidelines. I sat in the lobby at the UN when Peter Hansen, the director of the UN group dealing with transnational corporations, came out of negotiations with a small group of important leaders. He said, "Esther, our opponents are willing to approve the guidelines if we drop the sections on food, water, and pharmaceuticals."

"Over my dead body," came my reply. To take out those provisions would have made the guidelines nothing more than an empty shell. Sure, the guidelines would have passed, but they would have been meaningless. Big business wanted no interference with their operations; they wanted to be free to exploit workers and consumers and the natural resources of other countries, if they wished. They seemed to think they deserved complete autonomy, even though they weren't willing to behave responsibly.

At times the battle became almost amusing. My opponents charged that I was a foreign agent, working through an office in the Hague, the location of the central office of IOCU. They charged that my loyalties were no longer with the US. Unlike the time that Oliver's loyalty to the US was questioned, I never took these remarks seriously; it was all a joke to me.

The Department of Justice told me I was acting as a "foreign agent" and I needed to file with the US attorney general. It was really a way of stalling a meeting with Virginia Knauer, the special assistant to the president for consumer affairs at the time. She was in a tight spot: She could not represent consumers honestly and object to the guidelines, but politically she could not support them either. Consumers Union printed up buttons for my grandchildren and supporters saying, "Grandma is a foreign agent." In the end, these silly charges really helped me on Capitol Hill because they were so laughable.

Although it was clear that the Reagan administration opposed the guidelines because many multinational corporations didn't want them, the formal US objection was that the guidelines could interfere with international trade. What the guidelines would really do is improve product quality in developing countries and increase international competition. In any case, safety, health, and basic human rights should never be sacrificed to the marketplace.

One of the most outspoken critics of the guidelines was Murray Weidenbaum, director of the Center for the Study of American Business at Washington University of St. Louis. In an article titled, "The Case Against the Guidelines," he called the guidelines "a model of vagueness and overblown phraseology" and said they were another step toward the UN becoming a "Global Nanny." I later wrote to him about his inaccuracies, and at least I got him to admit that he had been wrong on some points. The same journal that published his original article published mine, titled, "The Case Against the Case Against the Guidelines."

The guidelines were adopted by the General Assembly in April 1985, and they have already had a significant impact on a number of developing countries. Uruguay took the guidelines as a starting point in its review of national legislation, eventually resulting in the creation of a National Board of Consumer Protection. Ecuador established a similar agency. In 1987 IOCU sponsored a regional meeting of 20 countries in Latin America and the Caribbean to discuss how to set up consumer protection groups. The systems are already working. There have been consumer groups formed in Bangkok, Poland, and Africa. The idea is yeasty; that is, it's coming along.

Several years after the guidelines passed, however, there was still talk of the ineffectiveness of voluntary standards. But a representative from Venezuela stood up at the General Assembly and said, "I thought that the Consumer Guidelines and the Consolidated List were just ideas, but they have made a big difference in my country. You can never underestimate the moral strength of taking a position, even if the position is voluntary." That really made me feel that our efforts had made a difference.

After the guidelines passed, I began work on the third component of the triad of global consumer protections, the United Nations Code of Conduct on Transnational Corporations, which may be renamed Guidelines on Overseas Investments because some countries are sensitive about the use of the word "code." The code establishes voluntary guidelines on how multinational corporations and host countries should conduct themselves in the world of international finance. They're designed to help corporations act as "good corporate citizens."

The code would set standards of decency, honesty, and fair competition across national boundaries. It would help US businesses by securing a stable environment for foreign investors. And, more important, because the practices would be part of an international agreement, businesses would be able to compete on a level playing field with other countries around the world.

In part, the code would protect foreign consumers by restricting a company's right to set high prices in one area (where the company has a monopoly) to offset unfairly low prices in another area (where the company wants to create a monopoly). The code as discussed by the General Assembly also would set ground rules for direct foreign investment and establish processes for consumer redress. It would ask that companies comply with the consumer and environmental protection laws and regulations in the countries where they operate. Companies would be required to clean up the environmental messes they make.

The standards aren't excessive or unfair; they're the same standards as those in effect in the US and other developed countries. We live in an interdependent world, and no nation—not even one as powerful as the US—can afford to live in isolation.

The benefits of the code are clear. Consider the 1984 Bhopal tragedy. If the code had been in effect and observed, Union Carbide and the Indian authorities might have observed certain environmental standards and disclosure requirements. While there's no way of knowing what might have been, the code's jurisdictional provisions would have clarified which court had authority and could have helped the victims receive prompt compensation.

The code has been debated since 1977. It began as an industry-bashing instrument designed to rein in the powerful multinational corporations that had enough money to dominate the governments in Third World countries just emerging from colonial domination. In some cases, a single multinational corporation called the shots and all but owned certain countries.

After 15 years of struggle, the code has become a cooperative venture. Today agreement has been reached on almost all the parts dealing with corporate and host country behavior. The sticking point has been getting approval on the details, especially the legal semantics. For example, should the code refer to international "law" or international "obligations"?

Many corporations already follow guidelines set up by The World Bank and other financial institutions that lend money for foreign investment. The problem is that there is no central set of guidelines. It's now such a hodgepodge; we need one set of rules. Once the rules are clear, it will become increasingly difficult for companies to justify not following them.

The US opposition to the code has been so vigorous at times that it has spilled over into what I consider to be unethical actions. In 1991 I went to the UN office to get the specifics on the US objections to the code. I was given a copy of a statement prepared by the State Department that had been sent to the US embassies around the world. The memo said the code was "not balanced" and listed the official objections— all of which had been addressed through modifications in the code— and it outlined how government officials might try to persuade foreign countries to join the opposition. It actually urged US diplomats to "quietly build a consensus against further negotiation at this time."

These underhanded tactics paid off. In 1992 the code was killed in a meeting of the Commission on Transnational Corporations. Instead, a mild resolution was passed recommending that the issue be looked at again in the next session. This is a small victory when you realize that we had achieved agreement on about 80% of the code. But we have not given up the fight.

Some people feel the UN should be only a peacekeeping organization where countries can talk instead of fight; they believe the UN has no business meddling in social and economic issues. I disagree.

I think consumer issues have a significant impact on international relations. After all, when workers are exploited, national resources are squandered, and human rights come in second to corporate greed, we cannot be surprised to find hostility between countries. International respect and economic cooperation are the foundations of peace.

In a sense, multinational corporations represent America abroad much more powerfully and visibly than striped-pants government officials and diplomats in US embassies. When US multinationals exploit foreign workers, pollute the environment in other countries, and sell unsafe or inferior quality goods with the "Made in the USA" label, they are putting a black mark on our country. We deserve better.

Chapter 11

Looking Back

When I left the White House in 1980, I was asked if I was considering retirement. It's something I'm always talking about, but I'm not sure that I ever will retire so long as I can feel useful. When I left the White House, I decided to do some volunteer lobbying on issues that I care about, such as pension reform, the rights of women, migratory workers, and the underprivileged. Since then, I have worked closely with the Older Women's League to help fight for and enhance the rights of middle-aged and older women in society. I helped organize the United Seniors Health Cooperative, a group that helps use senior power to bring about discounts on a vast array of consumer products. In 1988 I was hired as consumer adviser to the National Association of Professional Insurance Agents. I brought together consumer groups and insurance agents for the purpose of persuading state governments to approve minimum standards for financing, structuring, and staffing the civil departments that regulate the insurance business.

I would like to devote more time to joining the fight for universal health insurance. We have got to do something for the 40 million people who are left out. We also have to provide help with long-term care. People want to be at home. They don't want to go to hospitals. We must develop a policy in this country to make it possible for the disabled to stay at home and receive the help they need. There are big gaps in our health care system. The need for home care services is great, and such in-home medical and social services are extremely important. I learned that lesson years ago when I was living in Sweden. Nobody there is left isolated. Help is always available there for those who need it. We care about the dollar in this country, not the person, and I think that this is just inexcusable.

Obviously, women's issues are very important to me. We have made great strides with women's rights but we still have far to go. Women's jobs are traditionally low paying because we've never put value on work that's done in the home. The work women have done—teaching and nursing, for example—is an extension of the things they do for their families. It is just as skilled as the work men have always done. Women also have special problems as consumers. They make 70% of the nation's household purchasing decisions. These days, most women work, so they have a double or triple role to play. The least we can do is give them information on which to make their judgments. I think it is exciting, however, to see the progress that we've made. One of my granddaughters is talking about being president some day.

When I became involved in union work, I encountered the brave women who participated in the famous "Heartbreaker Strike." I met working women from the sweatshops and maids from the wealthy homes. I learned something about the conditions they faced and the absence of any rights or fair labor standards. I took an oath to myself that I would do something about their plight. This oath did not end with these women; it has carried me forward throughout the rest of my life.

Unlike my grandchildren, I didn't intentionally set out to follow a set career path; I just did what came naturally. Now, looking back, I can appreciate the interconnectedness of my activities, the way the themes of my life seem to join one experience with the next.

This feeling of one experience overlapping another really came into focus for the first time when I toured India in the late 1960s as a representative of the US Information Service, spreading the gospel of the free enterprise system and making speeches about labor, the women's movement, and consumer affairs. When traveling, I always peeked behind the scenes, beyond the boundaries of my official itinerary. I wanted to see where the workers lived, where they ate, where they slept, where they shopped, where they worked. Once I understood the people's lives, the rest of the city just seemed to fall into place.

I asked for a tour of a clothing factory in India. I had been around sweatshops, so I expected what I saw: scores of women hunched over sewing machines, sweating out a living for themselves and their families. The only real differences between the sweatshops I helped organize in New England and those in New Delhi were the nationality of the workers, and the bright colors and flowing fabric of the saris the Indian women wore. Despite the similarities, I didn't expect to see a familiar face.

When I met the foreman of the shop, our eyes locked in recognition. I knew the man, but I couldn't put him in context. For a moment, I stared at him, and he stared back. When he reached me he said, "Esther, what are you doing here?"

In a flash I remembered our first encounter 40 years before at a shirt factory in Troy, New York, where I was organizing for the Amalgamated Clothing Workers.

"I'm here to organize," I said with a smile.

"Oh, my God."

It seemed hard to believe that four decades had gone by and the issues were still the same—women were working for low wages in lousy conditions to make button-down shirts for conservative American men. I had been part of the labor movement as it grew more powerful during the New Deal days of the 1930s. In some cases, when the unions were established, businesses left town and set up "runaway" shops in other areas. When the Amalgamated started organizing the factories in New England, the companies shifted more work to New York and New Jersey where unions for women were not strong. When the unions caught up with them there, the companies moved south, then west, then overseas. Business always tried to stay one step ahead of organized labor, but the unions followed, at least to the US border.

In both the United States and India, most of the workers I saw in the factories were women, women who depended on wage work to support their families. I'll never forget hearing from the delegate from India at a meeting of the International Confederation of Free Trade Unions in 1949 about how difficult it was for some of these women to get by. Now I saw it firsthand. I noticed a folded napkin in one woman's lap.

"What does she have in her lap?" I asked.

"Food."

The foreman then explained that the company had been providing the women with food during the workday because they were so hungry that their productivity suffered. But rather than eat the food, the women would wrap it up and sneak it home so that they could give it to their children. The company tried to establish a policy that all food had to be eaten at work, but on occasion some of the women tried to smuggle uneaten food home to their families.

The problem, both in India and in the United States, is that many employers refuse to pay a living wage, a wage high enough for a worker to support his or her family. Most employers will do virtually anything to save money, so they cut corners on wages. It's hard to cut costs on machinery, so it's almost always the human being, the worker, who pays the price. That was true in the 1930s, and unfortunately it's still true today.

Through my experiences in the United States and dozens of other countries around the world, I have learned a few things about how people get along. I am an old lady in my ninth decade of life, and I believe I still have a lot to give. You don't have to stop contributing when your hair turns white; in fact, you may have more to give if you're able to build on your experiences and your past.

I feel strongly about the involvement of the elderly in all aspects of society. I think the elderly are going to be not only a political force, but also an ethical force. Our seniors must play a role in restoring the basic values of our society. It is our job to remind our young people that there is more to life than the individual pursuit of happiness. We must do our best to help others. I would like to see us do what they do in Sweden and other countries, where older people are found on public boards and given the responsibility to make decisions rather than being put out to pasture. I think Gray Power is a coming reality and I wouldn't be a bit surprised to see older people appointed to the Cabinet. The government has already made a great deal of investment in these older people and their talents should not be wasted.

I have found that, to stay vital all your life, you've got to stay involved. There's no question about that. You've got to be curious. You've got to be doing things. I do not want to join what they call the rocking chair set. That's all right for other people, but not for me. I believe in choice and I choose to be involved.

It's important that old people maintain the natural curiosity that they had as children. Seniors sometimes lose that quality, and I blame television a little bit. We get this spoon-fed culture without having to think about it much. We don't sit around the dining table as a family any more and discuss problems. The way you show love today is to take your family out to dinner. I like having the family around, sharing the meal, learning what has happened to everyone during the day, what problems were created and what problems were solved. It's this kind of bonding that makes a family strong. I think we miss a lot of that today.

It is important for me here to pay tribute to my heroes and mentors. My lobbying efforts between 1945 and 1948, which helped expand coverage for the Fair Labor Standards Act, guaranteeing a minimum wage and maximum working hours for American workers, put me in contact with one of my lifelong heroes. It was at that time that I first met Senator Claude Pepper.

It was my responsibility to lobby for the Fair Labor Standards Act. I felt very strongly about bringing all people under the umbrella of labor standards. Claude Pepper felt the same way. He had a wonderful rapport with the common man. I remember that his hearings were different in the sense that he insisted on taking testimony from ordinary folks as well as experts. I helped him get witnesses to testify. He always had an eye on making things better for those people who were left out or forgotten by our society. We have to begin to let people know who our heroes are. He certainly was one of mine.

Next in my personal pantheon is Eleanor Roosevelt. I would be honored to be mentioned in the same breath with her. I remember her as a warm, friendly, easy person. We used to go over to her place at Val Kil when I was working with the disadvantaged, and she would open her home to us. We would bring in people from the ghetto and the sweatshops, and would sit around having tea and singing. She was never above anyone. She was always with us. She could always communicate with whomever she was talking to, connecting the little problems that they were having and fitting them into a pattern of larger legislative issues. She had a wonderful skill. I was proud to work with her on the President's Commission on the Status of Women. Mrs. Roosevelt knew the importance of what we were doing. She said to me, "This may be the last big thing that I do in my life."

Mrs. Roosevelt has been a wonderful role model for me. I would like to walk a little bit in her shadow. Her work continues to inspire me and when things get rough and I wonder what I should do, then I say to myself, "Esther, remember Mrs. Roosevelt is standing behind you. She is by your side. Let's do it the way she would do it." This gives me the courage to go forward. It is almost spiritual.

Two US Senators from Utah also had a strong impact on my life. The first was Elbert Thomas, a former college professor and a marvelous person who wanted very much to help people, but was not always adept at translating issues in the way that they could be understood by the common man. The second was Senator Frank E. Moss, whom I helped win election to the Senate. He is a wonderful man. He has tremendous courage. He was one of those people who was always willing to stand up for what he thought was right. He had great integrity and wisdom. He was chair of the Consumer Affairs Subcommittee of the Senate at the time when I was special assistant to President Kennedy. Can you imagine my joy in having Senator Moss in the same field, knowing him as well as I did and knowing that we shared common ideals? It was wonderful. He helped me achieve many of the victories that were won during this time.

Next I would list Jimmy Carter. In 1977 President Carter reappointed me to the post of special assistant to the president for consumer affairs, a job I held through 1980. I remember Jimmy Carter fondly. He is just a superb human being. I worked with him on the senior staff of the White House and saw him in action. Over and over again, he would stand up for what he thought was right. People would ask him to take positions out of political expediency, but again and again I saw him refuse. It was difficult, but he did what was right. He worked so hard. If you sent him a memo at night, it would be back by 7:30AM with notes written in the margin. I think he will go down in history as a great president.

One of the greatest honors of my life was bestowed on me by President Carter in 1980 when he awarded me the Medal of Freedom. I always felt that it was a privilege just to be able to hold the jobs I have held and to have a chance to work on programs that I believe in. At that time, my active years in government were coming to a close, and I felt that my accomplishments and contributions were appreciated. I only wish that my Oliver would have been able to share the honor with me.

When I consider all the important jobs I have had and things I have done, one accomplishment overshadows all others: the fact that Oliver and I raised four wonderful children. My children—Karen, Eric, Iver, and Lars—are my greatest gift to the world. My children are my immortality. I feel that I will live on through them; this is a very Mormon belief.

I have not been an ideal Mormon. I moved east, drank coffee, played cards, and married a socialist who smoked a pipe—but I always lived by the principles that remain the foundation of the church. Throughout my life, I have honestly tried to follow my own code of ethics—one that was formed by my parents and the Mormon hymns I sang as a girl. I challenged—but did not abandon—the moral code of the church during my years as an activist. And so, when other people ask me, "Are you a good Mormon?" I must smile and reply, "This is my life, now you decide."

Sure, over the years I made a lot of enemies and alienated a lot of people in the power structure—both in government and in the Mormon Church. I did what I thought was right (and let the consequences follow), but after years of being considered an agitator and an outsider, I feel relieved to be accepted for who I am.

It may be that I am less threatening now that my braids are thin and white, or it may be that I have proved myself and defended my professional integrity over the years, but I have at last been accepted by the old-boy network. In 1988 I was one of the first women invited to join the Cosmos Club, an exclusive club for Washington's elite.

More important than my acceptance by the Cosmos Club has been my acceptance and warm welcome back in my home state of Utah. Though I've spent nearly half a century in Washington, DC, I've always considered Utah my home. In the past few years I've been invited back a number of times to make speeches and receive awards. I am proud to have been named to the Beehive Hall of Fame, one of the highest honors in Utah. At last my state has claimed me and affirmed that I belong.

For so long I felt that I did not fit in. When I was a young woman, so many of my neighbors and friends in Utah considered me a lost cause for having lived my life the way I did. These people assumed that my work came before my family, but they never knew me well.

My family has always been my source of strength. I have many happy memories of my parents and grandparents. They made each one of us children feel special. It made no difference if you were a boy or a girl; we were all to get educated, which was a little unusual in those days. Many of my earliest childhood memories also involve working alongside my parents. We all worked on our farm and other farms. I worked in the summer, picking fruit and helping earn my way. It was good work and it was hard work. I know about stooped labor, because I've done it. I picked cherries, apples, strawberries, and peaches. A good deal of the money I earned to fund my college education came from picking fruit.

Many of my fondest memories involve family recreation, which in that time meant sitting at the dining table reading the classics. We didn't have television in those days. We used to sit around the dining table and put up fruit or make our own rugs, and while we were doing this, Father would read to us. He read Balzac and Thoreau and the Greek philosophers. Some nights we would stop our work to discuss what he had read.

Education was always very important in my childhood household. My parents had profound respect for education. They had a very strong desire to see us learn. Learning was the undercurrent of everything that we did. Like my parents, I believe firmly in the importance of education. A weak educational system is a national tragedy. It is not only a great waste of undeveloped human talent, but it is harmful to the nation, which is governed by the will of the people. Our kind of government depends on an informed citizenry. Its people must be well grounded in our traditional ideals and values and must be sufficiently skilled to play their part in the nation's economy. Unless the fact is driven home that we live in an industrial society and must prepare ourselves accordingly, we cannot long expect our country to maintain its high standard of living and its high standard of moral leadership in the world.

What is the best thing our schooling gives us? Isn't it the wisdom to choose wisely? For life is a constant screening of choices between the good and the bad, between quantity and quality, between the frivolous and the serious. In a sense, life is like a trip through a king-sized supermarket filled with all sorts of temptations, deceptions, pretty promises, and solid values. The result is that we often find ourselves making choices without really knowing what the possible choices are and what is the proper basis for a decision. We even choose when we don't do something. For example, if we don't do anything to adjust educational processes to our changing minds, in effect we cast our vote for the status quo.

I have been asked what advice I would offer to young people of today. I say, first, that education is terribly important. Second, I think you've got to be involved. You have to be a participant in life, not an observer. Third, I think you have to learn to flow with the tide. I am thinking of Huck Finn as he drifts down the river saying, 'Well, let's glide down and see what's around the bend.' I'll never forget that quote. It almost epitomizes what I feel about life. I'm not one who feels that you have to be brave and be a star, but your life can be satisfying and happy if you work to make a difference. Maybe the difference will be just a little tiny piece and not a big difference. But the point is to make a difference by the way you live your life.

I want people to believe. I want them to care. I want them to be curious. I want them to look at injustice and ask, What can I do about that? I want them to know that they can certainly make a difference.

One of my favorite poems is by Bonarro Overstreet:
You say the little efforts that I made will do no good.
They never will prevail,
To tip the hovering scale,
Where justice hangs in balance.
I don't think I ever thought they would.
But I am prejudiced beyond debate,
In favor of my right to achieve which side shall deal
With several ounces of my weight.

Finally, if I'm remembered, I would like to be remembered as a nice old grandma. I would like to be remembered as Esther. I would like to be remembered as a kind, loving person who loved my family and people very much. I would like to be remembered as somebody who did what they liked to do and found satisfaction in doing it. That makes for a great deal of happiness in the end. Living is the thing that's important. It is the doing of things. I learned that from Mrs. Roosevelt. You don't do things because of the rewards or because someone may remember you after you are gone. The satisfaction is in the doing. Whether or not someone remembers does not really matter.

Another of my favorite poems is by Susan Barry, and it reads:
If you go the unusual way,
And if you stick your head out a little bit,
You might have a little trouble,
But the view is awfully good.

Thank you for taking this journey with me. If a little of my life's choices and conundrums have touched you, I wish you dispatch in turning your feelings into positive action for your own good and that of those whose lives you touch now and will touch in the future. We are all connected; there is no escape, as Booker T. Washington said: "We drag each other down, or lift each other up." There are no other choices. Look around you, at your companions on this journey, and choose to lift them up.